The Best Pasta Machine Cookbook Ever

The Best Pasta Machine Cookbook Ever

Brooke Dojny
and
Melanie Barnard

A John Boswell Associates/King Hill Productions Book

HarperCollins*Publishers*

HarperCollins books may be purchased for educational, business, or sales promotional use. For information please write: Special Markets Department, HarperCollins Publishers, Inc., 10 East 53rd Street, New York, NY 10022.

FIRST EDITION

Designed by Barbara Aronica
Index: Maro Riofrancos

Library of Congress Cataloging-in-Publication Data

Dojny, Brooke.
    The best pasta machine cookbook ever / by Brooke Dojny and Melanie Barnard. —1st ed.
      p. cm.
    "A John Boswell Associates/King Hill Productions book."
    Includes index.
    ISBN 0-06-017335-1
    1. Cookery (Pasta)   2. Pasta products.   3. Pasta machines.   I. Barnard, Melanie.   II. Title.
TX809.M17D64   1997
641.8'22—dc20

97   98   99   00   01   HC   10   9   8   7   6   5   4   3   2   1

Contents

Introduction

Until very recently, fresh pasta was a gourmet item, rarely found outside high-priced specialty food stores. But, as we Americans expand our love affair with pasta, and as we realize that grains, including pasta, are a mainstay of a nutritious diet, the demand for all kinds of pasta increases. Fresh pasta, in particular, has great appeal because of its very freshness, but also because it allows for all sorts of imaginative and innovative flavorings, colorings, and uses.

So it is absolutely no surprise that pasta machines, which allow us to make terrific fresh pasta at home, have great appeal. Even though myriad brands of fresh pasta are now supermarket staples, they are still limited in flavors, and remain on the high end of expensive. On the one hand, making pasta at home costs practically nothing. A pound of homemade egg fettuccine, for example, calls for nothing more than 3 cups of flour and 3 eggs—mere pennies. On the other hand, a pound of fresh fettuccine in the market could set you back several dollars.

In Italy, pasta is enjoyed both fresh and dried. But because fresh pasta travels poorly across the Atlantic, most of the imported pasta in this country has been of the dried variety. It is what we have become accustomed to, and it is what we have demanded of our own pasta producers as well. But as more Americans travel to Italy and enjoy fresh pasta, we now request it at home. Add to this our newly discovered love of noodles from Asia, an area that some people believe is the home of pasta anyway, and it is clear that we have not only incorporated pasta into our diet, we have made it a favorite food across the country. Now, besides cooking up all manner of classic sauces, innovative Americans sauce the noodle in ways never known in Italy or in Asia.

In fact, until now all of our effort and imagination has been centered on sauces, with the pasta itself a bland vehicle for other flavors. With today's new nutritional knowledge, pasta all by itself is, and should be, a main event in our diet, not just the underpinnings of a heavy sauce cloak. With its negligible fat content and its popular appeal, pasta has become the deserving star.

And that is precisely what made us try electric pasta machines. They promise unlimited possibilities for flavored pastas. And they deliver.

We are by nature not very mechanical (suffice it to say that we do not program the VCR). So, it was with a bit of skepticism and trepidation that we approached the electric pasta machine.

The machines seemed simple enough—a mixing container with a rotating paddle for kneading, an opening for the pasta to be extruded, and a set of circular dies or disks with perforations of various sizes and shapes. For all of the machines we tested, the dry ingredients are put into the mixing container, the machine started, and the wet ingredients simply poured slowly into the container. With the desired die attached, we were told that was all there was to it. (That's what they said when we got our VCR, too.)

So we followed the directions, then watched and waited. Within a few minutes, something began to happen in the area of the extruding die. Little dribs began to crank out. Then, they started to look like pasta—and like the pasta shape we had designated. What they didn't tell us was that we needed to be ready for all this. As the machine cranked, we rushed to keep up with the output. With one hand holding onto the linguine, we craned across the kitchen to retrieve a box of wax paper. These culinary gymnastics finally accomplished, we now had a place to gently lay out our cache of pasta as it continued to be extruded.

After several more minutes, the dough in the mixing container had exhausted itself, and the pasta was done. The pound of linguine was neatly reclining on the wax paper on the counter. We were amazed, and our imagination began to run riot with the possibilities. We could make lemon yellow pasta, pasta colored red with tomatoes, orange with carrots, green with spinach, even speckled with herbs. We could make our pasta taste like pesto, like Cajun spices, and even like jalapeño peppers. We might even make chocolate pasta. There would be no limit!

Getting Started

Since all of the pasta machines that we tested operate on essentially the same principles, the following is a general guide to using your machine, no matter what the make and model. However, each manufacturer best knows the intricacies and idiosyncrasies of its machines, so it makes great sense to read and follow the instructions in your manual first and foremost.

We assume you have now read the manual and have taken the pasta maker out of the box. Note that assembly is a rather simple and straightforward affair. The mixing container fits into a slot, the lid has a place to pour in liquid, and the extruder die can easily be secured in place. The machine either has a switch or a sliding stopper that changes the action from mixing and kneading to extruding. Depending upon your sauce choice, either make the pasta first or while the sauce is cooking. Remember that fresh pasta takes only minutes from start to finish.

Making Fresh Pasta

For consistency, most of our pasta recipes are geared to produce about 1 pound of pasta in an electric pasta machine and use 3 cups of flour. As a general rule, the amount of liquid per cup of flour is about ¼ cup. One "large" egg measures a scant ¼ cup, so egg pasta recipes are usually 3 cups flour and 3 eggs. If your machine has a larger or smaller capacity, simply adjust the recipes so that you are using the ratio of 1 cup flour to ¼ cup liquid.

Note, however, that even with this general rule of thumb, each batch will have slight variations in the dry to wet ingredient ratio. Even though they may all be graded "large," each egg is different. Flours vary, and even the humidity can be a determining factor. Finally, the pasta type is a variable, too. Thin capellini requires slightly more moisture than sturdier rigatoni, for example. All our recipes adjust the moisture where necessary with small amounts of water or other liquid.

Some machine manuals advise weighing all the ingredients. This does give greater accuracy, but since not everyone has a scale, we have developed our recipes using the standard dry and liquid measures.

Dry herbs are added with the flour, and other flavorings, vegetables for color, and a touch of oil are added with the liquids. If you are rolling homemade pasta by hand or using a hand-crank roller machine, the proportions of dry to liquid ingredients will be slightly different, so you may need to adjust the recipe a bit.

To begin, measure the dry ingredients. We use the scoop and level method of measuring, then sift the dry ingredients directly into the mixing container. In our opinion, sifted dry ingredients seem to mix and extrude better.

If using eggs in the pasta, break them into a liquid measuring cup, then add any other liquid to measure a total of ¼ cup per 1 cup of flour used—usually a total of ¾ cup liquid. Do not beat the eggs until the accurate measurement has been gauged, since beating aerates them, which appears to add volume.

Now, soak the die that you plan to use to cut the pasta shape in a bowl of very hot tap water with about 1 teaspoon of oil for about 1 minute. This little trick really makes for much easier pasta extrusion. Secure the die onto the machine and start up the motor.

Slowly pour the liquid into the mixing container, then allow the pasta to mix as directed in the machine's manual. Before you begin to extrude the pasta, check for the proper texture. This is really important, since pasta that is too dry or too wet will not extrude properly and will strain the machine's motor as well. (If you hear the machine begin to groan or strain, as if it begins to feel very warm, turn it off immediately.)

We have found that the best way to test for the proper dough consistency is to stop the machine and feel the dough. It should be moist, in small, walnut-size clumps that hold together when pressed but are not sticky. If the dough looks granular like cornmeal and crumbles when you try to form a small clump, it is too dry. Start the machine again and add water by tablespoonfuls, allowing about 1 minute of kneading between additions until the proper consistency forms. If the dough is in big, damp clumps that cling to the mixing blade, it is too wet. Start the machine and sprinkle in flour by tablespoons, kneading it in until the proper consistency forms. Note that it is harder to knead in more flour than it is to knead in more liquid, so it is better to err on the dry side in the original dough mixture. Though you may have a couple of troublesome batches at first, you will quickly become accustomed to mixing the right dough consistency for your machine.

Have ready a large piece of wax paper or a kitchen towel, then begin the extrusion process. At first, the dough will appear to be a bit ragged and uneven as it extrudes, especially through finer disks, such as the capellini cutter. Use a small sharp knife and an upward cutting motion to cut off and discard these initial efforts.

As the dough begins to extrude smoothly, guide it out with your hands. Cut it off at desired intervals using an upward motion with your knife, which assures cleaner cuts and pasta that does not stick together. Lay the pasta out on the wax paper or kitchen towel. In general, we find that cutting the pasta at about 12-inch intervals is easiest. When making macaroni or other short, stubby pasta, allow the long pieces to dry about 3 minutes on the wax paper, then cut them into the desired lengths. This short period of drying helps to keep the ends of the macaroni from sealing together when cut.

To help prevent stickiness, let the pasta air dry for at least 15 minutes before cooking or storing.

Cooking Fresh Pasta

Bring a large pot of water to a boil. We recommend about 4 quarts for every pound of pasta to be cooked. Salt the water and then return the water to a rapid boil. Commercial dry pasta and some commercial fresh pasta have no salt added, so well-salted water is needed for good cooked pasta flavor. One of the advantages of making your own pasta is controlling the flavor yourself and matching it to the sauce as well. We find that regular, unflavored Semolina Pasta is best when the dough is unsalted, so that it can be a basis for nearly any sauce. But when we began to experiment with dough flavorings, the pasta itself seemed to need salt, too. Our recipes reflect this, so our pasta cooking water is lightly salted. You may, of course, adjust the salt in both the pasta and the water according to your preference; you may even omit it entirely.

Do not overcook the pasta. Drop the pasta into a pot of rapidly boiling water. Use a long-tined fork to briefly mix and separate the pasta in the water. Then begin timing. Perfectly fresh pasta cooks in 1 to 5 minutes, depending upon the shape and size. If the pasta has been refrigerated or frozen, we recommend allowing it to stand at least 15 minutes at room temperature before cooking. Cold pasta added to boiling water greatly reduces the water temperature and thus delays the return to a boil and promotes the stickiness that occurs at lower temperatures.

Drain the pasta into a colander or large strainer, shaking off all excess moisture. Unless a specific recipe directs, do not rinse the pasta before using.

Cooking Times for Fresh Pasta

Capellini (angel hair)	1 to 2 minutes
Linguine	2 to 3 minutes
Fettuccine	2 to 3 minutes
Egg Noodles	2 to 3 minutes
Asian Noodles	2 to 3 minutes
Gnocchi	2 minutes
Spaghetti	2 to 3 minutes
Thick spaghetti	3 to 4 minutes
Small macaroni	3 to 4 minutes
Large macaroni (rigatoni, penne)	3 to 5 minutes
Lasagne	2 minutes
Tortellini	3 to 4 minutes
Ravioli	5 minutes

Storing Fresh Pasta

If you are not planning to cook the pasta within a few hours of making it, then it should be stored in the refrigerator or freezer.

Long-strand pasta is best stored in "nests." As the pasta is extruded, cut it into desired lengths, then lay it flat on the wax paper. Sprinkle the pasta lightly with cornmeal or semolina flour and toss gently with your fingers to be sure the strands are separated. Coil the pasta into loose nests. Let stand about 15 minutes, then refrigerate or freeze in sturdy plastic bags.

Macaroni or tubular pasta should be dried a little longer before storing. Setting pasta on a wire cake rack, which allows air circulation all around, promotes more even and thorough drying. Lightly sprinkle the pasta with cornmeal or semolina flour and store in sturdy plastic bags.

Fresh egg pasta can be refrigerated for about 24 hours or frozen for up to 3 months. Return the pasta to cool room temperature before cooking. When the stored pasta is cooked, the cornmeal or flour coating will keep the strands from sticking together and will drop off the strands as they cook.

Cleaning Up

If you remember the fun of making dough as a child, you will also remember that there is a small price to pay—the cleanup. Making fresh pasta involves cleaning the mixing bowl, kneading apparatus, and the extrusion die. We have learned a few tricks to make this much easier.

Disassemble the pasta machine as soon as you are finished extruding the pasta. (If you are making more than one batch of pasta at a sitting, be ready to make the second one immediately or the dough from the first will begin to harden and clog up the extruder.) Soak all of the parts except the extruding die and the machine itself in warm, soapy water. Do not soak the die, or the dough will soften and "cook" into a sticky mess. Wipe the machine itself clean with a damp cloth.

Manually remove excess pasta from the unwashed die, then allow it to sit on the counter for at least 2 hours or for up to 12 hours (or freeze for about 15 minutes) until the remaining dough dries and hardens. Then tap the die on the counter and most of the dried dough should flake off. Brush off any dried dough still clinging to the die. Depending upon the machine (check the manual), the die may or may not be now washed in the dishwasher. Unless your machine comes with a die-cleaning tool, which looks like a dull-edged push pin, do not attempt to clean the die holes with anything sharper than a wooden toothpick. Sharp points can damage the dies.

About Pasta Machines

Most electric pasta machines operate on similar principles. Some are more powerful and have a larger capacity than others. Prices vary and are often discounted. The following are some of the more readily available makes and models.

Creative Technologies Corporation—CTC makes several models of pasta machines. All have a switch that changes the action from mix to extrude.

The Pasta Express (Models X2000 and X3000) is among the easiest of machines to assemble and disassemble since the die fastens to the machine by means of a front plate with 2 easily adjusted knobs. The motor is powerful and produces about 1½ pounds of pasta. There are 8 pasta dies, a bread stick, a bagel, and a cookie die. Optional dies are available. There is a 12-month limited warranty.

Model X500 comes with the same capacity, dies, and options as the Pasta Express. The machine differs primarily in the method of die assembly; the die is fastened with a single knob that is best loosened by using the wrench that accompanies the machine. There is a 6-month limited warranty.

Cuisinart—The Cuisinart Deluxe Pasta Maker (Model DPM-3) features a really powerful direct-drive motor that seemed to be able to knead and extrude the dough especially well. A removable shutter slide allows the mixed dough to enter the extruding area. This machine comes with six very sturdy dies for pasta and one for bread sticks as well as a booklet with very clear instructions. There is an 18-month limited warranty.

Popeil Pasta Products, Inc.—Popeil's Automatic Pasta Maker has a capacity of about 1 pound and features 10 dies for pasta making as well as one each for bagels and cookies. There is only one basic pasta recipe, but several for sauces. There is a 6-month limited warranty.

Rival—The Rival Pasta Chef (Model PM 1000) has nine standard pasta dies and one cookie die. The accompanying booklet has several clearly written recipes and instructions. The unit has plenty of power for its moderate capacity. There is a 1-year limited warranty.

Simac—The Simac PastaMatic MX700 is a very strong machine with a large, 1⅓-pound capacity. It has an excellent full-color instruction manual and a separate, equally good, recipe booklet. Mixing and extruding are differentiated with a shutter glide. Eight pasta dies and one cookie die are standard, with many optional dies available. There is a 1-year limited warranty.

Vitantonio—The Pasta Perfetto 900 by Vitantonio is a large-capacity machine that changes from mix to extrude with the turn of a knob. Included are 8 standard pasta dies. It carries a 1-year limited warranty.

Helpful Tips

- Read the instructions that come with your pasta machine.
- Have all the ingredients ready before starting. Pasta making is a quick process.
- Plan to clean up right away.

- Be prepared for a few flops at the beginning. It takes a couple of batches to develop a "feel" for the proper dough consistency.
- Use your imagination in developing new flavored pastas. Just be sure that flavor additions are very finely ground or are smooth liquids.
- Check out the baby food section of the market. Pureed vegetables are ideal for coloring and flavoring pasta dough.
- If your machine begins to strain or groan during the pasta-making process, turn it off immediately. The dough is probably too dry or not properly kneaded. Let the machine cool before trying again.

A Note About Our Recipes

In most cases, our pasta recipes yield about 1 pound of pasta, which is ample for 4 servings. The doughs are designed to be used in an electric pasta machine. If you hand roll or use a manual machine, add a bit more liquid to the basic dough, since additional flour will be added during the kneading and rolling process.

Along with the yield, we give a listing of the recommended shapes for all of the pasta doughs. This can be important since very sturdy pastas like Semolina Pasta do not do well with the capellini cutter, and some of the Asian noodles are too fragile for macaroni shapes.

We have paired up shapes and sauces that we think go particularly well together. However, you can easily mix and match to your own taste. Lasagne and stuffed pastas can be made from almost any of the doughs.

Asian noodles are somewhat different from Italian-type pastas and are generally interchangeable only within their own categories. Asians generally use only long-strand noodles or squares or circles of dough to encase wonton or dumpling fillings. The noodles are not flavored, but are distinctive because of the basic noodle ingredients themselves, such as buckwheat or rice flour.

Semolina Pasta

This is the type of pasta you buy when you choose imported dried. Semolina flour, ground from durum wheat, is also marketed as pasta flour. It is increasingly available in well-stocked supermarkets and in most specialty food shops. Semolina has the highest gluten content of any wheat flour, and thus makes a very sturdy, flavorful pasta, which holds up to assertive saucing.

Makes 1 pound; use for spaghetti, linguine, tubular macaroni, lasagne

---

3 cups semolina flour
½ teaspoon salt

About ¾ cup water
2 teaspoons olive or vegetable oil

---

1. Measure the flour by scooping it into a measuring cup and leveling it off with the back of a knife. Sift it into the mixing container of the pasta machine along with the salt.
2. Start the machine and slowly pour ¾ cup water and the oil into the mixing container. Process, adding additional water by tablespoons if needed, and extrude as directed in the machine's manual.
3. Spread the pasta out on wax paper or kitchen towels. Let dry for at least 15 minutes or for up to 8 hours before using. This pasta can be stored, covered, at room temperature for up to 3 days. It can also be frozen for up to 1 month.

Semolina Linguine with Classic Pesto Sauce

This heady, pungent sauce can be made in quantity when your garden overflows with basil. Then freeze it for a touch of summer all winter long.

4 Servings

---

1 recipe Semolina Pasta
2 cups packed fresh basil leaves
¼ cup pine nuts (pignoli)
½ teaspoon salt

3 garlic cloves
½ cup olive oil, preferably extra-virgin
½ cup grated Parmesan cheese
1 tablespoon butter, softened

---

1. Cut the pasta into linguine. Let dry on wax paper for at least 15 minutes before using.
2. In a food processor, place the basil, pine nuts, and salt. With the machine on, drop the garlic through the feed tube, then slowly pour in the oil. Process until smooth, scraping down the side of the bowl once or twice, about 1 minute. Add the cheese and butter. Process until well blended, about 20 seconds. Use immediately, refrigerate for up to 3 days, or freeze for up to 3 months.
3. Cook the linguine in a large pot of boiling salted water until tender but still firm, about 2 minutes. Drain in a colander. Toss the pasta with the sauce and serve.

Semolina Linguine with Garlic and Oil

A strand pasta is best with this simple but pungent Italian classic. Use large garlic cloves from a firm, snowy white head and chop them by hand for a really sparkling garlic flavor.

4 Servings

---

1 recipe Semolina Pasta
½ cup extra-virgin olive oil
2 tablespoons finely minced garlic
½ teaspoon salt

¼ teaspoon crushed hot pepper flakes
¼ teaspoon freshly ground black pepper
¼ cup chopped flat-leaf parsley

---

1. Cut the pasta into linguine. Let dry on wax paper for at least 15 minutes before using.
2. Cook the linguine in a large pot of boiling salted water until tender but still firm, about 2 minutes. Scoop out and reserve ¼ cup of the cooking water. Drain the pasta in a colander.
3. Meanwhile, in a small saucepan, heat the oil. Add the garlic and cook over medium-low heat, stirring constantly, until the garlic begins to turn golden, about 2 minutes. Stir in the salt, hot pepper, and black pepper. Immediately toss with the pasta, parsley, and reserved cooking water.

Semolina Linguine with Simple Marinara Sauce

Marinara, or mariner's sauce, has no seafood in it, but it is attributed to Italian fishermen who needed a quickly prepared tomato sauce on their boats. Because the sauce cooks so quickly fresh herbs make a real difference here.

4 Servings

---

1 recipe Semolina Pasta
2 tablespoons extra-virgin olive oil
2 garlic cloves, crushed through a press
3 (14½-ounce) cans diced tomatoes, flavored "pasta-ready" if desired, with their juices

½ teaspoon salt
½ teaspoon freshly ground pepper
¼ cup chopped flat-leaf parsley
¼ cup chopped fresh basil
Grated Parmesan cheese

---

1. Cut the pasta into linguine. Let dry on wax paper for at least 15 minutes before using.
2. Meanwhile, in a large saucepan, heat the oil. Add the garlic and cook over medium heat, stirring, for 1 minute. Add the diced tomatoes with their juices, salt, and pepper. Bring to a boil, reduce the heat to medium-low, and simmer, partially covered, until slightly reduced, about 25 minutes.
3. Cook the linguine in a large pot of boiling salted water until tender but still firm, about 2 minutes. Drain in a colander. Toss the pasta with the sauce, parsley, and basil. Sprinkle with cheese and serve.

Semolina Penne with 20-Minute Meat Sauce

You can make this hearty sauce as quickly as you can open a jar of bottled sauce, and it tastes so much brighter and richer with the addition of almost any fresh herb, though basil is our favorite.

4 Servings

---

1 recipe Semolina Pasta
1 pound meat loaf mixture of ground
    beef, pork, and veal *or* 1 pound
    ground chuck
1 medium onion, chopped
1 large garlic clove, crushed through a
    press
1 teaspoon dried oregano

½ teaspoon dried summer savory
½ teaspoon salt
½ teaspoon freshly ground pepper
1 (28-ounce) can crushed tomatoes in
    puree
1 (14½-ounce) can Italian-style stewed
    tomatoes
¼ cup chopped fresh basil

---

1. Cut the pasta into penne or other similar tubular shape. Let dry on wax paper for at least 15 minutes before using.

2. Meanwhile, in a large saucepan, cook the ground meat, onion, and garlic over medium-high heat, stirring often, until the meat is no longer pink, about 8 minutes. Drain off any excess fat.

3. Stir in the oregano, savory, salt, and pepper. Add the crushed tomatoes and stewed tomatoes. Bring just to a boil, reduce the heat to medium-low, and simmer for 10 minutes. Stir in the basil and simmer for 2 minutes.

4. Cook the penne in a large pot of boiling salted water until tender but still firm, 3 to 5 minutes. Drain in a colander. Toss the pasta with the sauce and serve.

Semolina Perciatelli with Arrabiata Sauce

Arrabiata means "enraged" in Italian, and this spicy sauce might strike some as angry. If you don't have a thick spaghetti, or perciatelli, cutter on your machine, use a penne or ziti disk.

4 Servings

---

3 tablespoons olive oil
1 medium onion, chopped
2 garlic cloves, crushed through a press
¼ cup chopped jarred hot cherry peppers
¼ cup chopped sun-dried tomatoes in oil
½ teaspoon dried oregano

2 (14½-ounce) cans diced tomatoes, with their juices
½ cup dry red wine
Salt
1 recipe Semolina Pasta
Grated Parmesan cheese

---

1. In a saucepan, heat the oil. Add the onion and garlic and cook over medium heat, stirring often, until softened, 3 to 5 minutes. Stir in the cherry peppers, sun-dried tomatoes, and oregano. Cook 30 seconds. Stir in the diced tomatoes with their juices and the wine. Reduce the heat to medium-low and simmer until slightly thickened, about 15 minutes. Season to taste with salt. Use immediately or refrigerate for up to 3 days.

2. Cut the pasta into thick spaghetti (perciatelli) or a long tube shape. Let dry on wax paper for at least 15 minutes before using.

3. Cook the perciatelli in a large pot of boiling salted water until tender but still firm, 3 to 4 minutes. Drain in a colander. Toss the pasta with the sauce. Sprinkle with cheese and serve.

Semolina Spaghetti with Bolognese Sauce

The secret of this classic, perhaps the best-known of all meat sauces, is a touch of cream to smooth and connect all the flavors. If your meat market offers a meat loaf mix of ground beef, pork, and veal, it can be used here.

4 Servings

1 recipe Semolina Pasta
2 slices of bacon, cut into 1-inch pieces
1 tablespoon olive oil
1 medium onion, chopped
1 carrot, chopped
1 celery rib, chopped
2 garlic cloves, crushed through a press
½ pound lean ground pork
½ pound lean ground beef
¼ pound lean ground veal
1 cup dry white wine
1 cup beef broth
1 (28-ounce) can Italian-style plum tomatoes in puree
1 (16-ounce) can Italian-style plum tomatoes, with their juices
½ cup heavy cream
Salt and freshly ground pepper

1. Cut the pasta into spaghetti. Let dry on wax paper for at least 15 minutes before using.
2. In a large saucepan, cook the bacon over medium heat until lightly browned, about 3 minutes. Add the oil, onion, carrot, celery, and garlic. Cook, stirring often, until softened, about 5 minutes. Add the pork, beef, and veal and cook, stirring often to break up any lumps, until the meats lose their pink color, about 5 minutes.
3. Add the wine, broth, tomatoes in puree, and tomatoes with their juices. Bring to a boil, mashing the tomatoes with the back of a spoon. Reduce the heat to low and simmer, uncovered and stirring occasionally, until reduced to a medium sauce consistency. Add the cream and simmer for 15 minutes. Season to taste with salt and pepper.
4. Cook the spaghetti in a large pot of boiling salted water until tender but still firm, about 2 minutes. Drain in a colander. Toss the pasta with the sauce and serve.

Old-Fashioned Semolina Spaghetti and Meatballs

4 Servings

2 tablespoons olive oil
1 medium onion, chopped
1 carrot, chopped
1 garlic clove, crushed through a press
1 (28-ounce) can crushed tomatoes in puree
1 (14½-ounce) can Italian-style stewed tomatoes
¾ teaspoon dried marjoram
¾ teaspoon salt

¾ teaspoon freshly ground pepper
1 pound lean ground chuck
1 egg
2 tablespoons milk
¼ cup seasoned dry bread crumbs
2 tablespoons grated Parmesan cheese
2 tablespoons finely chopped parsley
¾ teaspoon dried thyme
1 recipe Semolina Pasta

1. In a large saucepan, heat the oil. Add the onion, carrot, and garlic and cook over medium heat, stirring often, until softened, about 5 minutes. Add the crushed tomatoes, stewed tomatoes, marjoram, and ½ teaspoon each of the salt and pepper. Bring to a boil, reduce the heat to medium-low, and simmer for 10 minutes.

2. Meanwhile, in a mixing bowl, blend the ground chuck, egg, milk, bread crumbs, cheese, parsley, thyme, and remaining ¼ teaspoon salt and ¼ teaspoon pepper with your hands. Form into about 16 meatballs, each about 1½ inches in diameter. Drop the meatballs into the simmering sauce. Spoon the sauce over the meatballs, but be careful not to break up the meat. Simmer until the meatballs are firm and no longer pink in the center, 20 to 25 minutes. Skim off any fat that rises to the top.

3. Cut the pasta into spaghetti. Let dry on wax paper for at least 15 minutes before using. Cook the spaghetti in a large pot of boiling salted water until tender but still firm, 2 to 3 minutes. Drain in a colander. To serve, ladle the sauce over the pasta.

Semolina Spaghettini with Puttanesca Sauce

If you don't have a thin spaghetti cutter, make regular spaghetti. This pasta dough is too firm to pass through a capellini or angel hair cutter. Puttanesca is a concentrated, lusty, and somewhat salty sauce, so be sure to cook the pasta in very lightly salted water.

4 Servings

1 recipe Semolina Pasta
¼ cup extra-virgin olive oil
3 garlic cloves, crushed through a press
4 anchovy fillets
1 (28-ounce) can plum tomatoes in juice, drained
1 (14½-ounce) can diced tomatoes, with their juices

½ cup sliced black olives, preferably oil-cured
2 tablespoons drained small capers
1 teaspoon dried oregano
½ teaspoon crushed hot pepper flakes
⅓ cup chopped flat-leaf parsley

1. Cut the pasta into spaghettini or spaghetti. Let dry on wax paper for at least 15 minutes before using.
2. Meanwhile, in a large skillet, heat the oil. Add the garlic and cook over medium heat, stirring, for 1 minute. Add the anchovies and mash with the back of a spoon. Add the plum tomatoes and diced tomatoes with their juices. Mash the plum tomatoes with the back of a spoon. Add the olives, capers, oregano, hot pepper, and parsley. Bring to a boil, reduce the heat to medium-low, and simmer, uncovered, stirring often, until the sauce thickens, about 20 minutes.
3. Cook the spaghettini in a large pot of lightly salted water until tender but still firm, 2 to 3 minutes. Drain in a colander. Toss the pasta with the sauce and serve at once.

Basic Egg Pasta

This is probably the most versatile and widely used homemade pasta. Because of the egg content, it must be refrigerated or frozen.

Makes 1 pound; recommended for all pasta shapes

---

3 cups all-purpose or unbleached flour
½ teaspoon salt
3 "large" eggs

2 teaspoons olive or vegetable oil
Water

---

1. Measure the flour by scooping it into a measuring cup and leveling it off with the back of a knife. Sift it into the mixing container of the pasta machine along with the salt.
2. Break the eggs into a liquid measuring cup. Add the oil and enough water to make ¾ cup. Use a fork or small whisk to lightly beat the eggs.
3. Start the machine and slowly pour the liquid into the mixing container. Process, adding additional water by tablespoons if needed, and extrude as directed in the machine's manual.
4. Spread the pasta out on wax paper or kitchen towels. Let dry for at least 15 minutes or for up to 2 hours before using. The pasta can be stored in the refrigerator for up to 24 hours or frozen for up to 1 month.

Egg Fettuccine with Amatriciana Sauce

Though this sauce is spicy with hot peppers, it should also have a light and fresh feel, sort of like the weather in the Italian town of Amatrice, for which it is named. Pancetta can be found in most Italian markets and in the deli section of larger supermarkets.

4 Servings

---

1 recipe Basic Egg Pasta

2 tablespoons olive oil

1 medium onion, chopped

⅓ cup chopped pancetta (or lean salt pork)

2 (14½-ounce) cans diced tomatoes, with their juices

½ teaspoon crushed hot pepper flakes

¼ cup chopped flat-leaf parsley

Salt

¼ cup grated or shaved Romano cheese, preferably Pecorino Romano

---

1. Cut the pasta into fettuccine. Let dry on wax paper for at least 15 minutes before using.
2. Meanwhile, in a large saucepan, heat the oil. Add the onion and pancetta and cook over medium heat, stirring often, until the onion is softened, 3 to 5 minutes. Add the tomatoes with their juices and hot pepper. Reduce the heat to medium-low and cook until slightly reduced, about 10 minutes. Stir in the parsley and season to taste with salt.
3. Cook the fettuccine in a large pot of boiling salted water until tender but still firm, 2 to 3 minutes. Drain in a colander. Toss the pasta with the sauce. Sprinkle with the cheese and serve.

Nana's Chicken Egg Noodle Soup

6 Servings

1 chicken (about 3 pounds) cut into 8
    parts, plus neck and back
2 quarts water
4 cups chicken broth
3 carrots
2 celery ribs
½ cup parsley sprigs, stems and leaves
    separated
4 whole peppercorns

4 whole cloves
1 teaspoon dried thyme
1 teaspoon dried oregano
½ teaspoon salt
½ teaspoon freshly ground pepper
1 recipe Basic Egg Pasta
1 cup frozen green peas
¼ cup grated Parmesan cheese, plus addi-
    tional cheese for passing

1. In a large Dutch oven or soup pot, bring all of the chicken, water, and broth to a boil. Skim off any foam that rises to the top. Cut 1 carrot and 1 celery rib into 1-inch chunks and add to the pot. Tie the parsley stems, peppercorns, and cloves in a cheesecloth bag and add along with the thyme, oregano, salt, and pepper. Reduce the heat to medium-low, partially cover, and simmer until the chicken is tender, about 45 minutes. Remove the chicken from the pot and let it cool, then remove the meat from the bones in chunks. Skim off and discard the fat from the soup stock. Discard the spice bag.

2. Cut the pasta into medium noodles or fettuccine. Let dry on wax paper for at least 15 minutes before using.

3. Chop the remaining carrots, celery ribs, and the parsley leaves. Add to the soup and return to a boil. Cook until the vegetables are just tender, about 5 minutes. Add the noodles and peas and cook until the noodles are tender but still firm, about 2 minutes. Return the chicken to the pot and heat through, about 1 minute. Stir in ¼ cup cheese. Pass additional cheese separately.

Egg Noodles in Alsatian Choucroute Sauce

4 Servings

1 recipe Basic Egg Pasta
1 tablespoon vegetable oil
¾ pound cooked German or Polish sausage or good-quality smoked kielbasa
4 thin smoked pork chops or 4 thick slices of smoked ham
1 medium onion, chopped
½ pound Savoy cabbage, thinly sliced (about 3 cups)

½ cup dry white wine
½ cup chicken broth
¾ teaspoon dried thyme
¼ teaspoon caraway seeds
4 crushed juniper berries or 2 tablespoons gin
1 bay leaf, broken in half
½ teaspoon freshly ground pepper
¾ cup heavy cream
Salt

1. Cut the pasta into wide or medium noodles or fettuccine. Let dry on wax paper for at least 15 minutes before using.
2. Meanwhile, in a large skillet, heat the oil. Add the sausage and pork chops and cook over medium-high heat, turning once or twice, until golden brown, 8 to 10 minutes. (You may need to do this in batches, depending upon the size of the skillet.) Remove the meat from the pan and add the onion to the drippings. Reduce the heat to medium and cook, stirring often, until the onion is just softened, about 3 minutes. Add the cabbage and cook, stirring, for 1 minute. Add the wine, broth, thyme, caraway seeds, juniper berries, bay leaf, and pepper. Return the meats to the skillet, reduce the heat to low, cover, and cook for 20 minutes. Remove and discard the bay leaf.
3. Cook the noodles in a large pot of boiling salted water until tender but still firm, 2 to 3 minutes. Drain in a colander. Remove the meats from the pan, add the cream, and bring to a boil, stirring constantly. Add the pasta and toss with the sauce. Season to taste with salt. To serve, spoon the noodles onto plates and arrange the meats on top.

Egg Noodles with Dilled Swedish Meatballs

4 Servings

1 recipe Basic Egg Noodles
1 pound meat loaf mix of ground beef, pork, and veal
⅔ cup fresh light rye bread crumbs
1 medium onion, chopped
1 egg, beaten
3 tablespoons chopped fresh dill or 1 tablespoon dried

¾ teaspoon salt
¾ teaspoon ground white pepper
¼ teaspoon grated nutmeg
1½ tablespoons vegetable oil
¾ cup chicken broth
1¾ cups half-and-half or light cream
Dill sprigs, for garnish

1. Cut the pasta into wide or medium egg noodles or fettuccine. Let dry on wax paper for at least 15 minutes before using.
2. In a large mixing bowl, use your hands to blend the ground meat, bread crumbs, onion, egg, and half each of the dill, salt, white pepper, and nutmeg. Form into about 24 meatballs, each 1 to 1½ inches in diameter.
3. In a large skillet, heat the oil. Add the meatballs and cook over medium-high heat, turning often with tongs, until browned, about 8 minutes. Add the broth, reduce the heat to medium-low, and simmer for 10 minutes. Add the half-and-half and remaining dill, salt, pepper, and nutmeg. Raise the heat to medium-high and cook until the sauce is slightly reduced, about 5 minutes.
4. Meanwhile, cook the noodles in a large pot of boiling salted water until tender but still firm, 2 to 3 minutes. Drain in a colander. Spoon the meatballs and sauce over the pasta. Garnish with dill sprigs.

Egg Noodles with Rosy Paprikash Sauce

Paprika loses its potency and bright color after several months on the shelf, so check yours for freshness. Imported Hungarian paprika has a distinct flavor that is especially good here.

4 Servings

---

1 recipe Basic Egg Pasta
1 tablespoon butter
2 ounces smoked ham, diced (about ½ cup)
¼ cup finely chopped shallots
1 tablespoon paprika

1½ teaspoons caraway seeds
1 cup dry white wine
1 cup heavy cream
1 tablespoon Dijon mustard
Salt and freshly ground pepper

---

1. Cut the pasta into medium noodles or fettuccine. Let dry on wax paper for at least 15 minutes before using.
2. In a large frying pan, melt the butter. Add the ham and cook over medium-high heat, stirring often, until lightly browned, 3 to 4 minutes. Add the shallots and cook until softened, 1 to 2 minutes. Stir in the paprika and caraway seeds. Add the wine and bring to a boil. Reduce the heat to medium and cook, stirring often, until slightly reduced, about 4 minutes. Stir in the cream and mustard and simmer until slightly thickened, about 4 minutes. Season to taste with salt and pepper.
3. Cook the noodles in a large pot of boiling salted water until tender but still firm, 2 to 3 minutes. Drain in a colander. Toss the pasta with the sauce.

Low-Fat "Egg" Pasta

Liquid egg substitute makes a lovely golden pasta that cooks up like egg noodles, but without most of the fat or any of the cholesterol.

Makes 1 pound; recommended for all pasta shapes

---

3 cups all-purpose bleached or unbleached flour
¾ teaspoon salt

¾ cup liquid egg substitute
2 teaspoons vegetable oil
Water

---

1. Measure the flour by scooping it into a measuring cup and leveling it off with the back of a knife. Sift it into the mixing container of the pasta machine along with the salt.
2. Start the machine and slowly pour the egg substitute and oil into the mixing container. Process, adding additional water by tablespoons if needed, and extrude as directed in the machine's manual.
3. Spread the pasta out on wax paper or kitchen towels. Let dry for at least 15 minutes or for up to 2 hours before using. The pasta can be stored in the refrigerator for up to 24 hours or frozen for up to 1 month.

Low-Fat Turkey Chili with Macaroni

Ground turkey provides a lean alternative to ground beef. Because it is somewhat bland, it is especially good in dishes that have lots of flavor punch, such as this piquant chili.

4 Servings

---

1 recipe Low-Fat "Egg" Pasta
1 tablespoon vegetable oil
1 pound ground turkey
1 medium onion, chopped
2 large garlic cloves, crushed through a
    press
1 tablespoon chili powder

1 teaspoon ground cumin
2 (14½-ounce) cans stewed tomatoes, pref-
    erably Southwest-style
½ cup reduced-sodium chicken broth
2 tablespoons finely chopped fresh or pick-
    led jalapeño peppers
⅓ cup chopped cilantro

---

1. Cut the pasta into elbow macaroni or other tubular shape. Let dry on wax paper for at least 15 minutes before using.
2. In a large skillet, heat the oil. Add the turkey and onion and cook over medium heat, stirring often, until the turkey loses its pink color and the onion is softened, about 5 minutes. Add the garlic, chili powder, and cumin. Cook, stirring, for 1 minute. Add the tomatoes and broth, reduce the heat to medium-low, and simmer for 15 minutes. Add the jalapeños and ¼ cup of the cilantro and simmer for 5 minutes.
3. Cook the macaroni in a large pot of boiling salted water until tender but still firm, 3 to 4 minutes. Drain in a colander. Toss the pasta with the sauce. Sprinkle with the remaining cilantro and serve.

Low-Fat Fettuccine and Grilled Vegetable Salad

6 Servings

---

1 recipe Low-Fat "Egg" Pasta
1 small red bell pepper
1 small green or orange bell pepper
1 small, narrow Asian eggplant (about 6 ounces)
1 small zucchini
1 small yellow crookneck squash

2 tablespoons extra-virgin olive oil
⅔ cup slivered fresh basil
¼ cup crumbled Gorgonzola cheese
¾ cup bottled low-oil or fat-free Italian dressing
Salt and freshly ground pepper

---

1. Cut the pasta into fettuccine. Let dry on wax paper for at least 15 minutes before using.
2. Prepare a medium-hot fire in a barbecue or gas grill. Coat the grill rack with nonstick vegetable spray. Quarter the bell peppers. Cut the eggplant and both squashes into lengthwise slices slightly less than ½ inch thick. Rub the vegetables with the oil. Grill, turning once or twice, until the vegetables are softened and lightly browned. The peppers and eggplant will take 8 to 10 minutes; the squashes will take 5 to 8 minutes.
3. Cook the fettuccine in a large pot of boiling salted water until tender but still firm, 2 to 3 minutes. Drain in a colander.
4. In a large shallow bowl, toss the pasta with the basil, Gorgonzola, and all but 3 tablespoons of the salad dressing. Season to taste with salt and pepper and toss again. Arrange the vegetables on top of the pasta. Drizzle the remaining salad dressing over the vegetables. Serve warm or at room temperature.

Low-Fat Penne with Roasted Broccoli

Roasting vegetables gives them a far richer taste and character and greatly diminishes the need for oil in a sauce. Since so little cheese is added, use the best quality you can find.

4 Servings

---

1 recipe Low-Fat "Egg" Pasta
1 bunch of broccoli (about 1 pound)
2 tablespoons extra-virgin olive oil
1 red bell pepper, quartered
2 garlic cloves, chopped
1 cup reduced-sodium chicken broth

1 cup dry white wine
½ teaspoon dried oregano
2 tablespoons grated Romano cheese, preferably Pecorino Romano
¾ teaspoon freshly ground black pepper
Salt

---

1. Cut the pasta into penne or other similar short tubular shape. Let dry on wax paper for at least 15 minutes before using.
2. Preheat the oven to 500 degrees. Separate the broccoli into florets, saving the stems for another use. Brush the broccoli florets with 1 tablespoon plus 1 teaspoon of the oil. Arrange the broccoli and bell pepper quarters in a single layer on a baking sheet. Roast, turning once or twice, until softened and tinged with brown, about 15 minutes. Cut the pepper quarters into thin strips.
3. Meanwhile, in a medium skillet, heat the remaining 2 teaspoons of oil. Add the garlic and cook over low heat, stirring constantly, until softened, about 1 minute. Add the broth, wine, and oregano. Raise the heat to medium and boil until reduced by nearly half, about 6 minutes. Remove from the heat.
4. Cook the penne in a large pot of boiling salted water until tender but still firm, 3 to 5 minutes. Drain in a colander. Toss the pasta with the sauce, broccoli, and pepper strips. Add the cheese, black pepper, and salt to taste and toss again.

Whole Wheat Pasta

This ratio of whole wheat to white flour results in a light brown pasta with a delicate nutty flavor and a firm but still tender texture.

Makes 1 pound; use for spaghetti, linguine, tubular macaroni, lasagne

---

2 cups whole wheat flour
1 cup all-purpose bleached or unbleached
   white flour
½ teaspoon salt

2 "large" eggs
¼ cup low-fat or skim milk
2 teaspoons olive or vegetable oil
Water

---

1. Measure the flour by scooping it into a measuring cup and leveling it off with the back of a knife. Sift it into the mixing container of the pasta machine along with the salt.
2. Break the eggs into a liquid measuring cup. Add the milk, oil, and enough water to make ¾ cup. Use a fork or small whisk to lightly beat the eggs.
3. Start the machine and slowly pour the eggs and oil into the mixing container. Process, adding additional water by tablespoons if needed, and extrude as directed in the machine's manual
4. Spread the pasta out on wax paper or kitchen towels. Let dry for at least 15 minutes or for up to 2 hours before using. The pasta can be stored in the refrigerator for up to 24 hours or frozen for up to 1 month.

Whole Wheat Linguine with Caponata

4 to 6 Servings

¼ cup extra-virgin olive oil
1 small eggplant (about ¾ pound), peeled and cut into ½-inch dice
1 medium onion, thinly sliced
1 celery rib, thinly sliced
1 red bell pepper, thinly sliced
2 garlic cloves, crushed through a press
1 pound fresh plum tomatoes, seeded and coarsely chopped
¼ cup halved and pitted Greek or Sicilian olives

1 tablespoon red wine vinegar
1 teaspoon sugar
1 bay leaf, broken in half
1½ teaspoons dried thyme
¼ teaspoon crushed hot pepper flakes
3 tablespoons chopped fresh basil
3 tablespoons chopped fresh parsley
2 tablespoons drained small capers
Salt and freshly ground pepper
1 recipe Whole Wheat Pasta

1. In a large nonreactive skillet, heat the oil. Add the eggplant, onion, celery, and bell pepper and cook over medium heat, stirring often, until the vegetables begin to soften, 3 to 5 minutes. Add the garlic and cook 1 minute. Stir in the tomatoes, olives, vinegar, sugar, bay leaf, thyme, and hot pepper. Cover and simmer, stirring often, until the vegetables are very soft, about 20 minutes.
2. Stir in the basil, parsley, and capers. Simmer, uncovered, stirring often, until roughly half the liquid has evaporated, about 15 minutes. Remove and discard the bay leaf. Season to taste with salt and pepper. Use immediately or let cool and refrigerate for up to 3 days. Reheat before using.
3. Cut the pasta into linguine. Let dry on wax paper for at least 15 minutes before using. Cook the linguine in a large pot of boiling salted water until tender but still firm, about 2 minutes. Drain in a colander. Toss the linguine with the caponata and serve.

Whole Wheat Penne with Autumn Vegetables

4 Servings

1 recipe Whole Wheat Pasta
4 thick slices of bacon, cut into ½-inch
    dice
2 tablespoons extra-virgin olive oil
1 large onion, sliced
3 garlic cloves, crushed through a press
2 (14½-ounce) cans stewed tomatoes
1 cup vegetable broth (canned is fine)
1 large sweet potato (about 8 ounces),
    peeled and cut into ½-inch dice

1 (16-ounce) can cannellini beans,
    drained and rinsed
1½ teaspoons dried rosemary
1 teaspoon dried thyme
1 medium zucchini (about 8 ounces), cut
    into ½-inch dice
¼ cup grated Parmesan cheese
Salt and freshly ground pepper

1. Cut the pasta into penne or other similar short tubular shape. Let dry on wax paper for at least 15 minutes before using.

2. In a large saucepan, cook the bacon over medium heat until crisp, about 5 minutes. Remove the bacon with a slotted spoon and drain on paper towels. Add the oil and onion to the pan drippings. Cook, stirring often, until softened, about 5 minutes. Add the garlic and cook for 1 minute. Add the tomatoes, broth, sweet potato, cannellini beans, rosemary, and thyme. Cover, reduce the heat to medium-low, and simmer until the sweet potato is tender, about 8 minutes. Add the zucchini and cook, uncovered, until the zucchini is tender and the sauce is slightly thickened, about 5 minutes. Stir in half of the cheese and the bacon. Season to taste with salt and pepper.

3. Cook the penne in a large pot of boiling salted water until tender but still firm, 3 to 5 minutes. Drain in a colander. Toss the pasta with the sauce. Sprinkle each serving with some of the remaining cheese and serve.

Whole Wheat Spaghettini with Mustard Cream Printemps

Ham, leeks, and peas, punctuated with bright red bell pepper, take beautifully to this creamy mustard sauce. Whole Wheat Pasta has enough character to stand up to the potent grainy mustard, sometimes called Pommery or country-style Dijon.

4 Servings

1 recipe Whole Wheat Pasta
2 tablespoons olive oil
1 red bell pepper, cut into ½-inch dice
2 leeks (white and light green), thinly
   sliced
1½ cups diced smoked ham (about
   6 ounces)

3 tablespoons grainy Dijon mustard
2 tablespoons chopped fresh tarragon or
   2 teaspoons dried
½ teaspoon freshly ground pepper
2 cups light cream or half-and-half
1 cup frozen baby peas, thawed
¼ cup grated Parmesan chese

1. Cut the pasta into spaghettini or thin spaghetti. Let dry on wax paper for at least 15 minutes before using.

2. In a large skillet, heat the oil. Add the bell pepper, leeks, and ham and cook over medium heat, stirring often, until the vegetables are softened and the ham is golden, 4 to 5 minutes. Stir in the mustard, tarragon, pepper, cream, and peas. Bring to a boil, reduce the heat to medium-low, and simmer until the sauce is slightly thickened, about 5 minutes.

3. Cook the spaghettini in a large pot of boiling salted water until tender but still firm, about 2 minutes. Drain in a colander.

4. Toss the pasta with the sauce. Sprinkle with the cheese, toss again, and serve.

Basil and Garlic Pasta

This is a highly seasoned pasta with a stand-out pesto flavor. It is particularly well suited to creamy sauces and to soups, such as Summer Minestrone (page 36).

Makes 1 pound; recommended for all pasta shapes except angel hair or capellini

---

3 garlic cloves, crushed through a press

1 tablespoon olive oil

3 cups all-purpose bleached or unbleached flour

½ teaspoon salt

3 "large" eggs

¼ cup finely chopped fresh basil

Water

---

1. In a small skillet or saucepan, cook the garlic in the oil over low heat, stirring constantly, for 1 minute. Let cool.

2. Measure the flour by scooping it into a measuring cup and leveling it off with the back of a knife. Sift it into the mixing container of the pasta machine along with the salt.

3. Break the eggs into a liquid measuring cup. Add the basil, garlic and oil, and enough water to make ¾ cup. Use a fork or small whisk to lightly beat the eggs.

4. Start the machine and slowly pour the liquid into the mixing container. Process, adding additional water by tablespoons if needed, and extrude as directed in the machine's manual.

5. Spread the pasta out on wax paper or kitchen towels. Let dry for at least 15 minutes or for up to 2 hours before using. The pasta can be stored in the refrigerator for up to 24 hours or frozen for up to 1 month.

Antipasto Pasta

Serve this simple but tasty dish warm or at room temperature. You can vary the ingredients according to your preference.

4 Servings

---

1 recipe Basil and Garlic Pasta
1 (7-ounce) jar marinated artichoke
   hearts
4 ounces thinly sliced salami, preferably
   Genoa, cut into thin strips
1 (6-ounce) jar roasted red peppers,
   drained and cut into strips

½ cup sliced black olives
1 medium red onion, finely diced
1 celery rib, thinly sliced
1 small yellow summer squash, sliced
¾ cup bottled Italian salad dressing, regular or fat-free
4 ounces fontina cheese, finely diced

---

1. Cut the pasta into penne or other similar shape. Let dry on wax paper for at least 15 minutes before using.

2. Drain the marinade from the artichoke hearts into a large mixing bowl. Quarter the artichoke hearts and add to the bowl along with the salami, roasted peppers, olives, red onion, celery, and squash.

3. Cook the penne in a large pot of boiling salted water until tender but still firm, 3 to 5 minutes. Drain in a colander. Add to the mixing bowl. Pour the salad dressing over the ingredients and toss to mix. Add the cheese and toss again. Serve warm or at room temperature.

Summer Minestrone with Basil and Garlic Pasta

There are as many versions of minestrone as there are Italian cooks. Most use short, stubby pasta. This one features ziti that is cut shorter than usual.

8 Servings

1 recipe Basil and Garlic Pasta
1 (5-ounce) piece of imported Parmesan
   cheese with its rind
¼ cup extra-virgin olive oil
1 large onion, chopped
1 celery rib, chopped
1 carrot, peeled and chopped
1 small green bell pepper, chopped
3 quarts chicken broth, preferably homemade or reduced-sodium
1 cup dry white wine
1 pound fresh plum tomatoes, seeded and
   diced, or 1 (14½-ounce) can diced tomatoes, with juices

2 cups fresh shelled and peeled fava beans
   or 1 (10-ounce) package frozen lima
   beans
2 teaspoons dried thyme
1 teaspoon dried summer savory
1 small zucchini, sliced
1 small head of Savoy cabbage, thinly
   sliced
¼ cup thinly sliced fresh basil leaves

1. Cut the pasta into a tubular shape, such as ziti, but cut the pieces ¾ inch long. Let the pasta dry on wax paper for at least 15 minutes before using. Cut the rind from the cheese and reserve. Grate the cheese.

2. In a large soup kettle, heat the oil. Add the onion, celery, carrot, and bell pepper and cook over medium heat, stirring often, until the vegetables are softened, about 5 minutes. Add the cheese rind, broth, wine, tomatoes, fava or lima beans, thyme, and savory. Bring to a boil, reduce the heat to medium-low, and simmer, uncovered, until the beans are tender, about 5 minutes.

3. Add the zucchini, cabbage, and pasta. Raise the heat to medium and cook until the pasta is tender but still firm, about 4 minutes. Remove and discard the cheese rind. Stir in the basil and grated cheese just before serving.

Basil and Garlic Linguine with Walnut and Mascarpone Sauce

This is undeniably a rich pasta sauce, but it is also undeniably delicious. It is also quick and easy to make.

4 Servings

---

1 recipe Basil and Garlic Pasta
1 cup coarsely chopped walnuts
8 ounces mascarpone cheese, at room
  temperature

¼ cup grated Parmesan cheese
⅓ cup milk, at room temperature
½ teaspoon salt
½ teaspoon freshly ground pepper

---

1. Cut the pasta into linguine. Let dry on wax paper for at least 15 minutes before using.
2. Preheat the oven to 350 degrees. Toast the walnuts in a single layer on a baking sheet, stirring occasionally, until lightly browned and fragrant, 5 to 7 minutes.
3. In a mixing bowl, stir together the toasted nuts, mascarpone, Parmesan cheese, milk, salt, and pepper until well blended.
4. Cook the linguine in a large pot of boiling salted water until tender but still firm, about 2 minutes. Drain in a colander. Gently toss the pasta with the walnut sauce and serve.

Basil and Garlic Fettuccine Alfredo

This is a reduced-fat version of an all-time favorite pasta dish. The flavored pasta adds an incomparable depth of flavor. Because the sauce is subtle, a really good cheese is important here.

4 Servings

---

1 recipe Basil and Garlic Pasta
2 tablespoons butter
¼ cup all-purpose flour
3 cups low-fat (1 or 2 percent) milk
¾ teaspoon salt

½ teaspoon freshly ground pepper
¼ teaspoon grated nutmeg
⅔ cup grated imported Parmesan cheese
2 tablespoons chopped flat-leaf parsley

---

1. Cut the pasta into fettuccine. Let dry on wax paper for at least 15 minutes before using.
2. In a medium saucepan, melt the butter over medium heat. Add the flour and cook, stirring, for 1 minute. Slowly whisk in the milk, then add the salt, pepper, and nutmeg. Bring to a boil, whisking constantly. Reduce the heat to medium-low and simmer, stirring often, for 5 minutes.
3. Meanwhile, cook the fettuccine in a large pot of boiling salted water until tender but still firm, 2 to 3 minutes. Drain in a colander. Toss the pasta with the sauce and the cheese. Sprinkle with the parsley and serve at once.

Basil and Garlic Manicotti with Mixed Meat Filling

For these scrumptious manicotti, delicate green basil and garlic pasta dough encases a smooth ground meat filling. The result is an elegant party dish that is as beautiful to look at as it is delicious to eat.

4 Servings

---

1 recipe Basil and Garlic Pasta
All-purpose flour
1 tablespoon butter
¾ pound meat loaf mix of ground beef, pork, and veal
1 small onion, chopped
½ teaspoon salt
¼ teaspoon freshly ground pepper

¼ teaspoon grated nutmeg
1 egg
2 tablespoons chopped parsley
1 cup heavy cream
2 cups coarsely chopped fresh or drained canned plum tomatoes
3 tablespoons grated Parmesan cheese

---

1. Cut the pasta into lasagne noodles about 7 inches long. Sprinkle lightly with flour and use a rolling pin or hand-cranked pasta machine to roll thinner (to between ⅟₁₆ and ⅛ inch thick). Trim the ragged edges and cut into 3-by-5-inch rectangles. You should have about 16 rectangles. Save any remaining pasta for another use. If not cooking the pasta immediately, dust it lightly with flour and wrap in plastic wrap, then refrigerate for 2 days or freeze for up to 1 month. Defrost in the refrigerator.

2. Cook the manicotti wrappers, about 8 at a time, in a large pot of boiling salted water until tender but still firm, about 2 minutes. Drain in a colander and run under cold water to cool. Drain on a kitchen towel until ready to use.

3. In a large skillet, melt the butter over medium heat. Add the ground meat and onion

---

Basil and Garlic Pasta

and cook, stirring often, until the meat loses its pink color, about 8 minutes. Season with the salt, pepper, and nutmeg. Transfer the meat mixture to a food processor and pulse to blend. Add the egg and parsley and pulse until fairly smooth.

4. Place the dough rectangles on a flat work surface and spoon 2 tablespoons of meat filling along the long edge of each manicotti; roll up. Place seam sides down in a lightly greased 9-by-13-inch baking dish. Bake immediately or cover and refrigerate for up to 8 hours. Return to room temperature before using.

5. Preheat the oven to 400 degrees. Pour the cream over the manicotti, scatter the tomatoes on top, and sprinkle on the Parmesan cheese. Bake, uncovered, in the preheated oven until the manicotti are heated through and the cream is bubbly, 15 to 20 minutes.

Baked Basil and Garlic Ziti with Roasted Potato and Tomato Sauce

4 Servings

2 tablespoons extra-virgin olive oil
2 leeks (white part only), thinly sliced
1 (14½-ounce) can Italian-style stewed
tomatoes
1¾ cups chicken broth
1 medium boiling potato, peeled and
finely diced
1 teaspoon dried oregano

½ teaspoon freshly ground pepper
¼ teaspoon salt
¼ teaspoon dried thyme
1 recipe Basil and Garlic Pasta
4 ounces thinly sliced or shredded mozzarella cheese
2 tablespoons grated Parmesan cheese

1. Preheat the oven to 350 degrees. In a 7-by-11-inch or other shallow 2-quart baking dish, combine the oil and leeks. Place in the oven for 5 minutes, stirring once. Add the stewed tomatoes, broth, potato, oregano, pepper, salt, and thyme. Stir to blend. Cover with foil and bake for 15 minutes. Uncover and bake until the sauce is slightly reduced and the potato is tender, about 30 minutes.

2. Meanwhile, cut the pasta into ziti or other tubular shape. Let dry on wax paper for at least 15 minutes before using. Cook the ziti in a large pot of boiling salted water until tender but still firm, 3 to 5 minutes. Drain in a colander. Stir the pasta into the sauce. (The casserole can be made a day ahead and refrigerated. Reheat, covered, in a 350 degree oven until heated through, about 20 minutes.)

3. Raise the oven temperature to 400 degrees. Sprinkle the mozzarella cheese over the top of the casserole, then sprinkle on the Parmesan cheese. Bake until the cheese is melted and bubbly, about 10 minutes.

Beet Pasta

Beet pasta is similar in color to Tomato Pasta but has a somewhat sweeter taste, brighter color, and more delicate texture.

Makes 1 pound; recommended for all pasta shapes

---

3 cups all-purpose bleached or unbleached
    flour
½ teaspoon salt
2 "large" eggs

¼ cup pureed cooked fresh or canned
    beets or baby food beets
2 teaspoons vegetable oil
Water

---

1. Measure the flour by scooping it into a measuring cup and leveling it off with the back of a knife. Sift it into the mixing container of the pasta machine along with the salt.
2. Break the eggs into a liquid measuring cup. Add the pureed beets, oil, and enough water to make ¾ cup. Use a fork or small whisk to lightly beat the eggs.
3. Start the machine and slowly pour the liquid into the mixing container. Process, adding additional water by tablespoons if needed, and extrude as directed in the machine's manual.
4. Spread the pasta out on wax paper or kitchen towels. Let dry for at least 15 minutes or for up to 2 hours before using. The pasta can be stored in the refrigerator for up to 24 hours or frozen for up to 1 month.

Beet Capellini with Scallops and Smoked Ham

4 Servings

1 recipe Beet Pasta
2 tablespoons butter
2 medium leeks (white and pale green), thinly sliced
2 ounces smoked ham, diced
½ cup chicken broth
¼ cup dry white wine
2 tablespoons lemon juice

¾ teaspoon grated lemon zest
1 teaspoon dried thyme
½ teaspoon freshly ground pepper
1 pound sea scallops
1 cup heavy cream
Salt
¼ cup chopped chervil or flat-leaf parsley

1. Cut the pasta into capellini. Let dry on wax paper for at least 15 minutes before serving.
2. In a large frying pan, melt the butter. Add the leeks and ham and cook over medium heat, stirring often, until the leeks are softened, about 5 minutes. Add the broth, wine, lemon juice, lemon zest, thyme, and pepper. Bring to a simmer. Add the scallops and simmer until just opaque throughout, about 3 minutes. Remove the scallops with a slotted spoon. Add the cream to the pan and boil until lightly thickened, 2 to 3 minutes. Season to taste with salt.
3. Cook the capellini in a large pot of boiling salted water until tender but still firm, about 1 minute. Drain in a colander. Toss the hot pasta with the sauce, scallops, and chervil and serve at once.

Red Flannel Fettuccine

The red in the classic Red Flannel Hash comes from beets. So we thought the other basic ingredients of corned beef and potatoes might be good with beet pasta. They are.

4 to 6 Servings

---

1 recipe Beet Pasta
4 slices of bacon
1 large onion, chopped
1 large boiling potato, peeled and cut into
 ½-inch dice
¾ pound cooked corned beef, cut into
 ½-inch dice

¼ cup chopped parsley
1½ cups half-and-half or light cream
1 tablespoon Worcestershire sauce
1 teaspoon Tabasco sauce
Bottled chili sauce

---

1. Cut the pasta into fettuccine. Let dry on wax paper for at least 15 minutes before using.
2. In a large skillet, cook the bacon over medium heat until crisp, about 5 minutes. Remove from the pan and drain on paper towels; crumble when cooled. Add the onion and potato to the drippings in the skillet and cook, stirring often, until the onion and potato are golden, about 8 minutes. Add the corned beef and cook for 2 minutes, stirring often. Add the parsley, cream, Worcestershire, and Tabasco. Reduce the heat to medium-low and simmer, stirring, until slightly thickened, about 5 minutes.
3. Cook the fettuccine in boiling lightly salted water until tender but still firm, 2 to 3 minutes. Drain in a colander. Ladle the hash over the fettuccine. Pass the chili sauce separately.

Beet Fettuccine with Creamy Ricotta and Kale

Other chopped greens, such as spinach and Swiss chard, can be substituted for the kale in this very pretty pasta dish.

4 Servings

---

1 recipe Beet Pasta
1 medium onion, chopped
3 tablespoons extra-virgin olive oil
2 garlic cloves, crushed through a press
1 pound fresh kale leaves, chopped, or
   1 (10-ounce) package frozen chopped
   kale, thawed
3 ounces thinly sliced prosciutto

1½ cups milk
1 cup part-skim ricotta cheese
1 teaspoon grated orange zest
½ teaspoon salt
½ teaspoon freshly ground white pepper
¼ teaspoon grated nutmeg
¼ cup grated Parmesan cheese

---

1. Cut the pasta into fettuccine. Let dry on wax paper for at least 15 minutes before using.
2. In a large skillet, cook the onion in the oil over medium heat, stirring often, until softened, 3 to 5 minutes. Add the garlic, kale, and prosciutto and cook, stirring often, until the kale is wilted, about 3 minutes. Stir in the milk, ricotta, orange zest, salt, pepper, and nutmeg. Cook, stirring, just until the sauce is heated through, 3 to 5 minutes. Stir in the Parmesan cheese.
3. Cook the fettuccine in a large pot of boiling salted water until tender but still firm, 2 to 3 minutes. Drain in a colander. Gently toss the pasta and sauce together and serve.

Black Pepper Pasta

The pepper gives the pasta an intriguing subtle taste and appearance. Use it to add zip to nearly any sauce.

Makes 1 pound; use for all pasta shapes except angel hair or capellini

---

3 cups all-purpose bleached or unbleached
    flour
1 tablespoon coarse or medium grind
    pepper

½ teaspoon salt
3 "large" eggs
2 teaspoons olive oil
Water

---

1. Measure the flour by scooping it into a measuring cup and leveling it off with the back of a knife. Sift it into the mixing container of the pasta machine along with the pepper and salt.

2. Break the eggs into a liquid measuring cup. Add the oil and enough water to make ¾ cup. Use a fork or small whisk to lightly beat the eggs.

3. Start the machine and slowly pour the liquid into the mixing container. Process, adding additional water by tablespoons if needed, and extrude as directed in the machine's manual.

4. Spread the pasta out on wax paper or kitchen towels. Let dry for at least 15 minutes before using. The pasta can be stored in the refrigerator for up to 24 hours or frozen for up to 1 month.

Cincinnati Chili Spaghetti

While Cincinnati Chili is always served over spaghetti, Black Pepper Pasta is definitely not found in any local chili parlor, but we think it adds a touch of class. For the uninitiated, the beans and cheese are optional.

4 to 6 Servings

1¼ pounds lean ground beef
2 medium onions, chopped
3 garlic cloves, crushed through a press
1½ cups beef broth
⅔ cup water
1 (14½-ounce) can diced tomatoes
1 (8-ounce) can tomato sauce
1 tablespoon cider vinegar
1 teaspoon Worcestershire sauce
2 tablespoons chili powder
1 teaspoon paprika
¾ teaspoon oregano

½ teaspoon ground cumin
½ teaspoon cayenne
¼ teaspoon salt
½ ounce (½ square) unsweetened
  chocolate
3 whole allspice berries
3 whole cloves
½ cinnamon stick
1 bay leaf, broken in half
1 recipe Black Pepper Pasta
1 cup each kidney beans and shredded
  Cheddar cheese

---

1. In a heavy 4-quart saucepan or Dutch oven, combine the meat, half of the onions, the garlic, beef broth, and water. Cover and cook over medium-low heat, stirring often and mashing the meat so that it doesn't clump, for 30 minutes. Spoon off any fat that rises to the top. Add the tomatoes, tomato sauce, vinegar, Worcestershire, chili powder, paprika, oregano, cumin, cayenne, salt, and chocolate. Tie the allspice, cloves, cinnamon, and bay leaf in a small cheesecloth bag and add to the pot, pushing it down into the chili. Partially cover and simmer over medium-low heat until thickened to a thick sauce consistency, about 1 hour. Discard the spice bag.

---

2. Meanwhile, cut the pasta into spaghetti. Let dry on wax paper for at least 15 minutes before using.

3. Cook the spaghetti in a large pot of boiling salted water until tender but still firm, 2 to 3 minutes. Drain in a colander.

4. To serve, ladle the sauce over the spaghetti in shallow serving plates. Top with the remaining onion. Pass the beans and cheese on the side.

Black Pepper Fettuccine with Roasted Garlic and Mussel Cream

4 Servings

6 garlic cloves, unpeeled
2½ tablespoons extra-virgin olive oil
1 recipe Black Pepper Pasta
1 small fennel bulb, chopped
2 medium leeks (white part only), thinly sliced
2 cups light cream

4 dozen mussels (about 4 pounds), scrubbed and debearded
1 cup dry white wine
1 cup clam juice
2 tablespoons Pernod or Ricard
⅓ cup chopped flat-leaf parsley

1. Preheat the oven to 400 degrees. Place the garlic on a small sheet of foil, drizzle with ½ tablespoon of the oil, and wrap loosely. Roast until the garlic is soft, about 30 minutes.
2. Cut the pasta into fettuccine. Let dry on wax paper for at least 15 minutes before using.
3. In a large skillet, heat the remaining 2 tablespoons oil. Add the fennel and leeks and cook over medium heat, stirring often, until softened, about 5 minutes. Squeeze the garlic cloves from their skins and add to the skillet. Add the cream and boil until reduced by about one-third, 6 to 8 minutes.
4. In a large pot, steam the mussels in the wine and clam juice until they open, 3 to 5 minutes. Reserve 8 of the best-looking mussels in their shells; remove the remaining mussels from their shells. Strain the cooking liquid into the skillet with the vegetables, taking care not to pour in the sediments in the bottom of the pan. Add the Pernod. Boil until reduced by about one-quarter, about 5 minutes.
5. Cook the fettuccine in a large pot of boiling salted water until tender but still firm, 2 to 3 minutes. Drain in a colander. Divide the pasta among 4 large, shallow soup plates. Reheat the cream sauce if necessary and add the mussels and parsley. Ladle the sauce over the pasta. Garnish with the mussels in their shells.

Black Pepper Linguine with Robust Red Clam Sauce

In New England, red clam sauces are usually very peppery. This shortcut version has a double hit, both in the sauce and in the pasta.

4 Servings

1 recipe Black Pepper Pasta
2 tablespoons olive oil
4 garlic cloves, crushed through a press
3 cups bottled marinara sauce, preferably with hot pepper added
¼ to ½ teaspoon crushed hot pepper flakes, to taste

1 cup drained chopped fresh clams, juices reserved, or 1 (10-ounce) can clams, drained with juices reserved
½ cup dry red wine
⅓ cup chopped flat-leaf parsley

1. Cut the pasta into linguine. Let dry on wax paper for at least 15 minutes before using.
2. In a large skillet, heat the oil. Add the garlic and cook over medium heat, stirring constantly, for 1 minute. Add the marinara sauce, hot pepper, juices from the clams, and the wine. Bring to a boil, reduce the heat to medium-low, and simmer for 15 minutes. Stir in the clams and parsley.
3. Cook the linguine in a large pot of boiling salted water until tender but still firm, about 2 minutes. Drain in a colander. To serve, ladle the sauce over the pasta.

Black Pepper Vermicelli with Bloody Mary Sauce

This sauce is pure fun and purely delicious. It begins with commercial Bloody Mary mix and adds a jolt of vodka or gin, depending upon how you like your Bloody Marys.

4 Servings

---

1 recipe Black Pepper Pasta
1 medium onion, chopped
2 celery ribs, thinly sliced
2 tablespoons olive oil
2 garlic cloves, crushed through a press
2 cups bottled Bloody Mary mix

1 (14½-ounce) can diced tomatoes, with their juices
⅓ cup gin or vodka
½ cup herb-seasoned croutons
½ to 1 teaspoon Tabasco sauce, to taste

---

1. Cut the pasta into vermicelli or thin spaghetti. Let dry on wax paper for at least 15 minutes before using.

2. In a medium saucepan, cook the onion and celery in the oil over medium heat, stirring often, until softened, about 5 minutes. Add the garlic and cook 1 minute. Add the Bloody Mary mix, tomatoes, and gin. Bring to a boil, reduce the heat to medium-low, and simmer, stirring occasionally, until reduced by one-third, about 15 minutes.

3. Cook the vermicelli in a large pot of boiling salted water until tender but still firm, about 2 minutes. Drain in a colander. To serve, ladle the sauce over the pasta. Sprinkle on the Tabasco and toss. Sprinkle the croutons on top.

Cajun Pasta

The intensity of flavor here will vary with the brand of Cajun or "blackened" spice mix that you use. You may have to fiddle around a bit with the amount and brand at first. The pasta should have a hint of Cajun herbs and spices, but not so much that it overwhelms the sauce.

Makes 1 pound; recommended for all pasta shapes

---

3 cups all-purpose bleached or unbleached flour
1 tablespoon Cajun or "blackened" spice blend

3 "large" eggs
2 teaspoons vegetable oil
Water

---

1. Measure the flour by scooping it into a measuring cup and leveling it off with the back of a knife. Sift it into the mixing container of the pasta machine along with the spice blend.

2. Break the eggs into a liquid measuring cup. Add the oil and enough water to make ¾ cup. Use a fork or small whisk to lightly beat the eggs.

3. Start the machine and slowly pour the liquid into the mixing container. Process, adding additional water by tablespoons if needed, and extrude as directed in the machine's manual.

4. Spread the pasta out on wax paper or kitchen towels. Let dry for at least 15 minutes or for up to 2 hours before using. The pasta can be stored in the refrigerator for up to 24 hours or frozen for up to 1 month.

Cajun Penne with Chunky Chicken Sauce Piquante

This roux-based sauce is such a favorite in Louisiana that a festival dedicated to Sauce Piquante is held every year in Raceland, Louisiana. In combination with Cajun pasta, it's sure to please those legions of folks who truly love spicy-hot dishes.

4 to 6 Servings

---

1 recipe Cajun Pasta
2 tablespoons vegetable oil
2 tablespoons all-purpose flour
1 medium onion, coarsely chopped
1 celery rib, chopped
1 medium green bell pepper, coarsely chopped
2 large garlic cloves, crushed through a press
1 (28-ounce) can whole tomatoes, drained and chopped
1 cup chicken broth

1 pickled jalapeño pepper, minced
2 bay leaves
1 teaspoon dried thyme
½ teaspoon salt
¼ teaspoon freshly ground black pepper
⅛ teaspoon freshly ground white pepper
⅛ teaspoon cayenne
1 pound skinless, boneless chicken breasts, cut into ½-inch dice
2 tablespoons red wine vinegar
4 scallions, thinly sliced

---

1. Cut the pasta into penne. Let dry on wax paper for at least 15 minutes before using.
2. In a large skillet or Dutch oven, heat the oil over medium heat. Add the flour and cook, stirring constantly, until the roux is golden brown, 3 to 5 minutes. Add the onion, celery, bell pepper, and garlic. Cook, stirring occasionally, until the vegetables are softened, about 5 minutes.
3. Add the tomatoes, chicken broth, jalapeño, bay leaves, thyme, salt, black pepper, white

pepper, and cayenne. Cook the sauce, uncovered, over medium heat until slightly thickened, about 8 minutes. Add the chicken and continue to cook until the meat is white in the center, about 8 minutes longer. Stir in the vinegar. Remove and discard the bay leaves.

4. Cook the penne in a large pot of boiling salted water until tender but still firm, 3 to 5 minutes. Drain in a colander. Toss the pasta with the sauce and sprinkle with the scallions before serving.

Cajun Fettuccine with French Quarter Shrimp Creole

4 to 6 Servings

---

1 recipe Cajun Pasta
2 tablespoons butter
1 large onion, chopped
1 celery rib, chopped
1 medium green bell pepper, chopped
3 garlic cloves, crushed through a press
1 (28-ounce) can whole tomatoes, drained
1 cup clam juice
1 teaspoon dried thyme

¾ teaspoon paprika
½ teaspoon salt
¼ teaspoon freshly ground black pepper
¼ teaspoon cayenne
2 bay leaves
1 pound large shrimp, shelled and
   deveined
4 scallions, thinly sliced

---

1. Cut the pasta into fettuccine. Let dry on wax paper for at least 15 minutes before using.
2. In a large skillet or Dutch oven, melt the butter over medium heat. Add the onion, celery, pepper, and garlic. Cook, stirring occasionally, until the vegetables soften, about 5 minutes.
3. Add the tomatoes, clam juice, thyme, paprika, salt, black pepper, cayenne, and bay leaves. Break the tomatoes up into smaller chunks with the side of a spoon. Cook, uncovered, over medium heat until the sauce is quite thick, about 25 minutes. Add the shrimp and cook until they are pink and curled, 3 to 4 minutes. Remove and discard the bay leaves.
4. Cook the fettuccine in a large pot of boiling salted water until tender but still firm, 3 to 4 minutes. Drain in a colander. Ladle the sauce over the hot pasta and sprinkle with the scallions before serving.

Cajun Spaghetti with Bayou Andouille Sauce

4 Servings

1 recipe Cajun Pasta
¾ pound andouille or other garlicky smoked sausage, such as kielbasa, cut into ¼-inch slices
2 tablespoons butter
1 large onion, chopped
1 large green bell pepper, chopped

3 garlic cloves, crushed through a press
1 (28-ounce) can crushed tomatoes with their juices
2 teaspoons dried thyme
1 teaspoon sugar
½ teaspoon freshly ground pepper
2 bay leaves

1. Cut the pasta into spaghetti. Let dry on wax paper for at least 15 minutes before using.
2. In a large skillet, cook the sausage over medium heat, stirring frequently, until lightly browned and some of the fat is rendered, about 5 minutes. Remove to a plate with a slotted spoon. Do not wash the pan.
3. Add the butter to the pan drippings. Add the onion, bell pepper, and garlic. Cook over medium heat, stirring occasionally, until softened, about 5 minutes. Add the tomatoes, thyme, sugar, black pepper, bay leaves, and ¾ cup of water. Reduce the heat to medium-low and simmer, uncovered, for 30 minutes, until the sauce is slightly thickened and the flavors are blended. Remove and discard the bay leaves.
4. Cook the spaghetti in a large pot of boiling salted water until tender but still firm, 2 to 3 minutes. Drain in a colander. Spoon the sauce over the spaghetti and serve.

Cajun Spaghettini with Crawfish Court Bouillon Sauce

If you're lucky enough to get fresh crawfish in your region, save any of the orange fat from the heads and add it to the sauce for extra flavor. If crawfish aren't available, substitute shrimp. The name for this Cajun dish is more than slightly confusing. In France, a "court bouillon" is a flavored poaching liquid; when it was transported to Louisiana, somehow it became a spicy red sauce for seafood.

4 to 6 Servings

1 recipe Cajun Pasta
3 tablespoons vegetable oil
3 tablespoons all-purpose flour
1 medium onion, chopped
1 medium green bell pepper, chopped
1 celery rib, chopped
6 scallions, thinly sliced
2 large garlic cloves, crushed through a
    press
1 cup clam juice
1 (16-ounce) can whole tomatoes, with
    their juices

½ cup dry white wine
1 tablespoon lemon juice
2 bay leaves
1 teaspoon dried thyme
½ teaspoon cayenne
½ teaspoon salt
½ teaspoon freshly ground black pepper
1½ pounds shelled crawfish tails or me-
    dium shrimp (see Note)

1. Cut the pasta into spaghettini. Let dry on wax paper for at least 15 minutes before using.
2. In a large heavy skillet or Dutch oven, heat the oil over medium heat. Add the flour and cook, stirring constantly, until the roux is pale golden, 3 to 4 minutes. Add the

onion, bell pepper, celery, scallions, and garlic. Cook, stirring occasionally, until softened, about 5 minutes.

3. Add the clam juice, tomatoes, and wine. Break up the tomatoes with the side of a spoon. Stir in the lemon juice, bay leaves, thyme, cayenne, salt, and black pepper. Reduce the heat to low and simmer, uncovered, until the sauce thickens, about 20 minutes.

4. Add the crawfish or shrimp to the sauce and simmer until the shellfish are pink and curled, 2 to 3 minutes. Remove and discard the bay leaves.

5. Cook the spaghettini in a large pot of boiling salted water until tender but still firm, about 2 minutes. Drain in a colander. To serve, toss the pasta with the sauce.

NOTE: Three pounds of crawfish tails in their shells will yield 1½ pounds shelled.

Carrot Pasta

Carrot gives pasta a fabulous sunny yellow color, which makes a beautiful palette with all sorts of green and red sauces. If you wish, add a chopped herb, such as tarragon, for a lovely, flavorful pasta that needs little more sauce than a little garlic and oil.

Makes 1 pound; recommended for all pasta shapes

---

3 cups all-purpose bleached or unbleached flour

½ teaspoon salt

2 "large" eggs

¼ cup pureed cooked fresh carrot or baby food carrots

2 teaspoons olive oil

Water

---

1. Measure the flour by scooping it into a measuring cup and leveling it off with the back of a knife. Sift it into the mixing container of the pasta machine along with the salt.

2. Break the eggs into a liquid measuring cup. Add the pureed carrot, oil, and enough water to make ¾ cup. Use a fork or small whisk to lightly beat the eggs.

3. Start the machine and slowly pour the liquid into the mixing container. Process, adding additional water by tablespoons if needed, and extrude as directed in the machine's manual.

4. Spread the pasta out on wax paper or kitchen towels. Let dry for at least 15 minutes or for up to 2 hours before using. The pasta can be stored in the refrigerator for up to 24 hours or frozen for up to 1 month.

Carrot Capellini with Parsley-Dill Pesto

Peanuts replace the usual pine nuts here, and dill stands in for the traditional basil in this delectable pesto that looks and tastes just right with Carrot Pasta.

4 Servings

---

1 recipe Carrot Pasta
⅔ cup packed flat-leaf parsley sprigs
½ cup packed fresh dill sprigs plus
    4 sprigs for garnish
½ cup roasted peanuts

2 garlic cloves
½ cup extra-virgin olive oil
2 tablespoons white wine vinegar
¼ cup chicken broth
Salt and freshly ground pepper

---

1. Cut the pasta into capellini. Let dry on wax paper for at least 15 minutes before using.
2. In a food processor, coarsely puree the parsley, packed dill sprigs, ¼ cup of the peanuts, and the garlic. With the machine on, slowly add the oil through the feed tube to make a smooth paste. Pour in the vinegar and broth and puree until smooth. Season to taste with salt and pepper. (The pesto sauce can be made up to 1 day ahead and refrigerated. Return to room temperature before serving.)
3. Finely chop the remaining peanuts. Cook the capellini in a large pot of boiling salted water until tender but still firm, about 1 minute. Toss the pasta with the pesto. Garnish with the remaining dill sprigs and the chopped peanuts.

Brunswick Stew over Carrot Noodles

4 to 6 Servings

1 recipe Carrot Pasta
¾ pound skinless, boneless chicken breasts
   or thighs, cut into 1-inch chunks
Salt and freshly ground pepper
3 tablespoons butter
1 onion, coarsely chopped
1 celery rib, thinly sliced
1 (14½-ounce) can stewed tomatoes
1 cup chicken broth

1½ teaspoons dried thyme
¼ teaspoon celery seed
1 cup frozen baby lima beans
1 cup fresh or frozen okra, sliced
¾ cup fresh or frozen corn kernels
1 tablespoon Worcestershire sauce
1 teaspoon Tabasco or other hot pepper
   sauce
2 tablespoons dry sherry

1. Cut the pasta into noodles or fettuccine. Let dry on wax paper for at least 15 minutes before using.

2. Season the chicken lightly with salt and pepper. In a large skillet, melt half of the butter over medium-high heat. Add the chicken and cook, turning often until golden, about 4 minutes. Remove the chicken from the pan. Add the remaining butter, reduce the heat to medium, and add the onion and celery. Cook, stirring often, until the vegetables are softened, about 5 minutes. Add the stewed tomatoes, broth, thyme, and celery seed. Bring to a boil, reduce the heat to medium-low, cover, and cook for 10 minutes. Add the lima beans and okra, cover, and cook for 5 minutes. Return the chicken to the skillet. Add the corn and simmer, uncovered, until the chicken is white throughout but still juicy, about 5 minutes. Stir in the Worcestershire, Tabasco, and sherry. (The stew can be made up to 1 day ahead and refrigerated. Reheat when ready to serve.)

3. Cook the noodles in a large pot of boiling salted water until tender but still firm, 2 to 3 minutes. Drain in a colander. Toss the chicken with the noodles and serve.

Peter Rabbit's Carrot Rigatoni

Peter Rabbit would love carrot pasta, especially with this sauce that includes all those other garden nibbles he craved so much. The Gorgonzola is for his friend Mickey.

4 Servings

---

1 recipe Carrot Pasta
6 tablespoons extra-virgin olive oil
1 red bell pepper, diced
4 garlic cloves, crushed through a press
½ cup vegetable broth
½ cup dry white wine
1 yellow summer squash, coarsely diced
1 cup sugar snap peas

½ cup thinly sliced scallions
1 tablespoon chopped fresh thyme or
  1 teaspoon dried
¼ cup thinly sliced radishes
1 cup crumbled Gorgonzola cheese (about
  4 ounces)
Salt and freshly ground pepper

---

1. Cut the pasta into rigatoni or other similar shape. Let dry on wax paper for at least 15 minutes before using.

2. In a large skillet, heat the oil. Add the bell pepper and cook over medium heat, stirring often, until the pepper is softened, about 4 minutes. Add the garlic and cook for 1 minute. Add the broth and wine. Bring to a boil and cook for 2 minutes. Add the summer squash, sugar snap peas, scallions, and thyme and cook until the peas are bright green and crisp-tender, about 2 minutes.

3. Cook the rigatoni in a large pot of boiling salted water until tender but still firm, 3 to 5 minutes. Drain in a colander. Toss the pasta with the sauce, radishes, and cheese. Season to taste with salt and pepper. Serve warm or at room temperature.

Carrot Ziti Ratatouille

4 Servings

1 recipe Carrot Pasta
1 large onion, thinly sliced
¼ cup extra-virgin olive oil
3 garlic cloves, crushed through a press
2 small zucchini, sliced
1 small eggplant (about ¾ pound), unpeeled and cut into ¾-inch dice
1 green bell pepper, thinly sliced
½ teaspoon salt
½ teaspoon freshly ground pepper

1 pound fresh plum tomatoes, seeded and
cut into ½-inch dice
½ cup dry white wine
1 tablespoon balsamic vinegar
1 tablespoon chopped fresh rosemary or
1 teaspoon dried
1 tablespoon drained small capers
2 ounces Pecorino Romano cheese in
1 piece

1. Cut the pasta into ziti or other similar shape. Let dry on wax paper for at least 15 minutes before using.

2. In a large skillet, cook the onion in the oil over medium heat, stirring often, until softened, 3 to 4 minutes. Add the garlic and cook for 30 seconds. Add the zucchini, eggplant, and bell pepper and stir to coat with the oil. Season with the salt and pepper. Cover the pan, reduce the heat to medium-low, and cook, stirring occasionally, until the eggplant is soft, about 25 minutes. Add the tomatoes, wine, vinegar, and rosemary. Cover and cook for 10 minutes. Add the capers and simmer, uncovered, for 3 minutes. (The ratatouille can be made 1 day ahead and refrigerated. Reheat to use.)

3. Cook the ziti in a large pot of boiling salted water until tender but still firm, 3 to 5 minutes. Drain in a colander. Toss the pasta with the sauce. Use a swivel vegetable peeler to shave thin slices of cheese over the pasta.

Cilantro Pasta

Cilantro is one of our favorite fresh herbs. It is important both in Latin American and Far Eastern cooking, making this pasta very versatile, indeed.

Makes 1 pound; recommended for all pasta shapes except angel hair or capellini

---

3 cups all-purpose bleached or unbleached
   flour
½ teaspoon salt
3 "large" eggs

¼ cup minced cilantro
2 teaspoons vegetable oil
Water

---

1. Measure the flour by scooping it into a measuring cup and leveling it off with the back of a knife. Sift it into the mixing container of the pasta machine along with the salt.
2. Break the eggs into a liquid measuring cup. Add the cilantro, oil, and enough water to make ¾ cup. Use a fork or small whisk to lightly beat the eggs.
3. Start the machine and slowly pour the liquid into the mixing container. Process, adding additional water by tablespoons if needed, and extrude as directed in the machine's manual.
4. Spread the pasta out on wax paper or kitchen towels. Let dry for at least 15 minutes or for up to 2 hours before using. The pasta can be stored in the refrigerator for up to 24 hours or frozen for up to 1 month.

Curried Squash and Pepper Cilantro Pasta Frittata

4 Servings

½ recipe Cilantro Pasta
2 tablespoons butter
1 medium red onion, chopped
1 small green bell pepper, coarsely
   chopped
1 medium yellow crookneck squash, thinly
   sliced
1 garlic clove, crushed through a press

1 teaspoon curry powder
¼ teaspoon ground cumin
¼ teaspoon ground coriander
½ teaspoon grated lemon zest
6 eggs
½ teaspoon salt
¼ teaspoon cayenne
1 cup shredded Swiss cheese

---

1. Cut the pasta into spaghetti. Let dry on wax paper for at least 15 minutes before using. Cook the pasta in a large pot of boiling salted water until nearly tender but still firm, about 2 minutes. (Slightly undercook the pasta for this dish since it will be further cooked in the frittata.)

2. Melt the butter in a large flameproof frying pan. Add the onion, bell pepper, and squash and cook over medium heat, stirring often, until the vegetables are tender, about 5 minutes. Stir in the garlic, curry powder, cumin, coriander, and lemon zest. Cook, stirring, for 1 minute.

3. In the mixing bowl, lightly beat the eggs with the salt and cayenne. Stir in the cooked pasta and pour over the vegetables in the skillet. Stir gently to combine.

4. Preheat the broiler. Cover the skillet and cook over low heat, stirring once or twice, until the eggs are almost set, about 10 minutes. Sprinkle the Swiss cheese over the frittata and set under the broiler about 4 inches from the heat source. Broil until the eggs are set and the cheese is bubbly, 1 to 2 minutes. Let stand for 2 minutes, then cut into wedges and serve directly from the skillet.

Cilantro Linguine with New Mexican Chorizo, Corn, and Chile Sauce

4 Servings

1 recipe Cilantro Pasta
1 tablespoon vegetable oil
½ pound chorizo or other spicy garlicky sausage, thinly sliced
1 medium onion, chopped
1 medium green bell pepper, chopped
1 or 2 fresh jalapeño peppers, seeded and minced
2 (14½-ounce) cans stewed tomatoes
1 (4-ounce) can chopped green chiles
½ cup chicken broth
1 cup fresh or frozen corn kernels
½ teaspoon grated lime zest
1 tablespoon lime juice
Salt
½ cup part-skim ricotta cheese
2 tablespoons chopped cilantro

1. Cut the pasta into linguine. Let dry on wax paper for at least 15 minutes before using.
2. In a large skillet, heat the oil. Add the chorizo, onion, and bell pepper and cook over medium heat, stirring often, until the sausage is browned and the vegetables are tender, about 5 minutes. Add the jalapeños and cook for 1 minute. Add the stewed tomatoes, green chiles, and broth. Bring to a boil, reduce the heat to medium-low, and simmer, uncovered, for 10 minutes. Add the corn, lime zest, and lime juice and simmer for 5 minutes. Season to taste with salt.
3. Cook the linguine in a large pot of boiling salted water until tender but still firm, about 2 minutes. Drain in a colander. Toss the linguine with the sauce. Divide among 4 plates or pasta bowls. Dollop each serving with a spoonful of ricotta. Garnish with the cilantro.

Southwest-Style Cilantro Lasagne

Chipotle chiles, which are suggested in this recipe, are brick-red dried and smoked jalapeño peppers that add a wonderful smokiness and heat to sauces and stews. They're packaged dried or in adobo sauce in cans and can be found in specialty markets and in many supermarkets. As is true for most of our baked lasagnes, if the noodles are very thin and fresh, they won't need boiling beforehand.

8 Servings

---

2 tablespoons olive oil

2 medium onions, chopped

2 green bell peppers, chopped

3 large garlic cloves, crushed through a
   press

2 tablespoons chili powder

1 teaspoon ground cumin

1 teaspoon dried oregano

1 (28-ounce) can chopped plum tomatoes,
   with their juices

1 diced chipotle chile (optional)

½ teaspoon salt

¼ teaspoon cayenne

½ cup chopped parsley

1 recipe Cilantro Pasta

3 cups part-skim ricotta

2 cups shredded Monterey Jack cheese with
   jalapeños

1½ cups shredded sharp Cheddar cheese

---

1. Heat the oil in a large skillet over medium heat. Add the onions, bell peppers, and garlic and cook, stirring often, until softened, about 5 minutes. Add the chili powder, cumin, and oregano and cook, stirring, for 1 minute. Add the tomatoes and chipotle chile. Simmer the sauce, uncovered, for about 20 minutes to blend the flavors. Remove the chipotle, chop fine, and return to the sauce. Season with the salt and cayenne and stir in the parsley.

2. Cut the pasta into lasagne noodles about 6 inches long. Use a rolling pin or hand-cranked pasta machine to roll out to a thickness of about ¹⁄₁₆ inch.

---

3. In a medium bowl, toss together the Monterey Jack and Cheddar cheese. Spoon 1 cup of the tomato sauce into a 3- to 4-quart shallow baking dish, tilting to coat the bottom. Layer with one-third of the pasta, trimming to fit if necessary, then half of the ricotta and one-third of the cheeses. Spoon one-third of the sauce over the cheese. Repeat the layering, ending with the last third of the pasta and sauce. Sprinkle with the remaining cheese. Cover with foil. If not using immediately, refrigerate for up to 24 hours. Return to room temperature before baking.

4. Preheat the oven to 350 degrees. Bake the casserole, covered, for 30 minutes. Uncover and bake until the lasagne is heated through and the cheese is melted, 15 to 20 minutes.

Susan's Baked Cilantro Macaroni and Cheese

Cookbook author Susan Wyler has a great macaroni and cheese recipe in her book Cooking from a Country Farmhouse. *We have adapted her recipe to our cilantro pasta.*

6 Servings

---

1 recipe Cilantro Pasta
3 tablespoons butter
2 tablespoons all-purpose flour
1 garlic clove, crushed through a press
2 cups milk
¼ teaspoon salt

¼ teaspoon cayenne
8 ounces extra-sharp Cheddar cheese, shredded
2½ teaspoons Dijon mustard
Crispy Crumb Topping (recipe follows)

---

1. Cut the pasta into macaroni. Let dry on wax paper for at least 15 minutes before using. Preheat the oven to 375 degrees. Butter a 14-inch oval gratin dish or a shallow 2-quart baking dish.

2. In a large saucepan, melt 2 tablespoons of the butter over medium-low heat. Add the flour and cook, whisking, for 1 minute. Add the garlic, then gradually whisk in the milk, salt, and cayenne. Raise the heat to medium and bring to a boil, whisking until smooth and thickened. Remove from the heat. Gradually stir in the cheese. Whisk in the mustard.

3. Cook the macaroni in a large pot of boiling salted water until almost tender, about 3 minutes. Drain in a colander. (It is good to slightly undercook the pasta for this dish since it will be further cooked in the oven.)

4. Add the macaroni to the cheese sauce and stir until mixed. Turn into the buttered baking dish. Sprinkle the Crispy Crumb Topping over the top and dot with the remaining 1 tablespoon of butter.

5. Bake, uncovered, until the sauce is bubbly and the top is golden brown, about 20 minutes. Let stand for about 5 minutes before serving.

Crispy Crumb Topping

Makes about 2 cups

4 slices of firm-textured white bread, torn
   into pieces
⅓ cup chopped shallots
⅓ cup coarsely chopped parsley
2 garlic cloves, crushed through a press
1½ teaspoons imported hot paprika or 1½
   teaspoons sweet paprika and several
   dashes of cayenne

¼ teaspoon salt
¼ teaspoon freshly ground pepper
2 tablespoons butter
1 tablespoon olive oil

1. Place the bread, shallots, parsley, garlic, paprika, salt, and pepper in a food processor. Process, pulsing the machine, to make coarse crumbs.
2. In a large skillet, melt the butter in the oil over medium heat. Add the seasoned crumbs and cook, stirring frequently, until the crumbs are toasted to a light golden brown and the garlic is fragrant, 3 to 5 minutes.

Cilantro Rigatoni with Pork and Black Bean Chili Sauce

Cilantro Pasta adds a light and fresh note to a hearty sauce such as this one. The chili is also good with Cornmeal Pasta.

4 Servings

---

3 tablespoons vegetable oil
1 pound boneless pork loin, cut into ½-inch cubes
1 medium onion, chopped
1 large garlic clove, crushed through a press
1 tablespoon chili powder
1 teaspoon ground cumin

1 teaspoon dried oregano
2 (14½-ounce) cans Mexican-style stewed tomatoes
1 (16-ounce) can black beans, drained and rinsed
Salt
1 recipe Cilantro Pasta

---

1. In a large saucepan, heat the oil. Add the pork and onion and cook over medium heat, stirring often, until the meat is lightly browned and the onion is softened, 5 to 7 minutes. Add the garlic, chili powder, cumin, and oregano. Cook, stirring, for 1 minute. Add the tomatoes, reduce the heat to medium-low, and simmer, partially covered, for 10 minutes.

2. Add the beans and simmer, partially covered, for 20 minutes. Season to taste with salt. (The chili can be made up to 3 days ahead and refrigerated. Reheat before using.)

3. Cut the pasta into rigatoni or other similar shape. Let dry on wax paper for at least 15 minutes before using.

4. Cook the rigatoni in a large pot of boiling salted water until tender but still firm, 3 to 5 minutes. Drain in a colander. Toss the pasta with the chili and serve.

Cornmeal Pasta

Use yellow cornmeal to give a pale golden hue and pleasantly gritty texture to the pasta.

Makes 1 pound; use for spaghetti, linguine, tubular macaroni, lasagne

---

2 cups all-purpose bleached or unbleached
    flour
1 cup yellow cornmeal
½ teaspoon salt

3 "large" eggs
2 teaspoons corn or vegetable oil
Water

---

1. Measure the flour by scooping it into a measuring cup and leveling it off with the back of a knife. Sift it into the mixing container of the pasta machine along with the cornmeal and salt.

2. Break the eggs into a liquid measuring cup. Add the oil and enough water to make ¾ cup. Use a fork or small whisk to lightly beat the eggs.

3. Start the machine and slowly pour the liquid into the mixing container. Process, adding additional water by tablespoons if needed, and extrude as directed in the machine's manual.

4. Spread the pasta out on wax paper or kitchen towels. Let dry for at least 15 minutes or for up to 2 hours before using. The pasta can be stored in the refrigerator for up to 24 hours or frozen for up to 1 month.

Cornmeal Fettuccine with Mighty Hot BBQ Shrimp Sauce

In New Orleans, barbecued shrimp are not barbecued at all, but are simmered in the shell in a searingly hot sauce. This same idea works well with Cornmeal Pasta, which can hold its own against all that heat.

4 Servings

---

1 recipe Cornmeal Pasta
6 tablespoons butter
2 teaspoons dried rosemary, crumbled
1½ teaspoons paprika
¼ teaspoon cayenne
1½ cups beer (12 ounces)

3 tablespoons lemon juice
1 tablespoon Worcestershire sauce
1 pound medium or large shrimp, shelled
  and deveined
¼ cup chopped parsley

---

1. Cut the pasta into fettuccine. Let dry on wax paper for at least 15 minutes before using.
2. In a large skillet, melt the butter with the rosemary, paprika, and cayenne over medium heat. Cook for 1 minute. Add the beer and boil until slightly reduced, about 5 minutes. Stir in the lemon juice and Worcestershire sauce. Add the shrimp and cook, stirring often, until the shrimp turn pink, 3 to 4 minutes.
3. Cook the fettuccine in a large pot of boiling salted water until tender but still firm, about 3 minutes. Drain in a colander. Spoon the shrimp and sauce over the pasta. Sprinkle the parsley on top and serve.

Crabmeat with Tomatillo Sauce and Cornmeal Linguine

4 servings

1 recipe Cornmeal Pasta
1 pound fresh tomatillos or 1 (10-ounce) can
3 tablespoons vegetable oil
1 medium onion, chopped
2 large garlic cloves, crushed through a press

1 to 2 fresh or pickled jalapeño peppers, minced
½ cup clam juice
½ cup dry white wine
⅓ cup chopped cilantro
½ pound lump crabmeat, picked over

1. Cut the pasta into linguine. Let dry on wax paper for at least 15 minutes before using.
2. Remove the papery brown husks from the fresh tomatillos. Cook in a large saucepan of boiling water until just tender, about 5 minutes. Drain well, let cool, and finely chop the tomatillos. (If using canned tomatillos, simply drain and chop.)
3. In a large skillet, heat the coil. Add the onion and cook over medium heat, stirring often, until softened, 3 to 5 minutes. Add the garlic and jalapeños and cook 1 minute. Add the clam juice and wine and boil, stirring occasionally, until slightly reduced, 2 to 3 minutes. Add the tomatillos and their juices and cook for 3 minutes. Stir in the cilantro and simmer for 1 minute.
4. Cook the linguine in a large pot of boiling salted water until tender but still firm, 2 to 3 minutes. Drain in a colander. Toss the hot pasta with the hot sauce. Add the crabmeat and toss gently just to combine, taking care not to break up the crabmeat.

Sante Fe Cornmeal Salsa Spaghetti

4 Servings

1 recipe Cornmeal Pasta
1 pound plum tomatoes, seeded and
  chopped (about 3 cups)
¾ cup thinly sliced scallions
2 garlic cloves, crushed through a press
1 to 2 fresh or pickled jalapeño peppers
½ cup bottled thick salsa

⅓ cup chopped cilantro
¼ cup extra-virgin olive oil
1 tablespoon red wine vinegar
¾ teaspoon salt
6 ounces diced Monterey Jack cheese, at
  room temperature

1. Cut the pasta into spaghetti. Let dry on wax paper for at least 15 minutes before using.
2. In a large mixing bowl, stir together the tomatoes, scallions, garlic, jalapeño peppers, salsa, cilantro, oil, vinegar, and salt. Let stand at least 15 minutes or for up to 2 hours at room temperature before using.
3. Cook the spaghetti in a large pot of boiling salted water until tender but still firm, about 3 minutes. Drain in a colander and return to the hot cooking pot. Add the sauce and cheese and toss until the cheese is partially melted, about 1 minute. Serve immediately.

Cornmeal Ziti with Turnip Greens 'n' Garlic

Cornmeal Pasta reminds us just a bit of corn bread, and that reminds us of one of our favorite Southern dishes—fried greens. And that's how this recipe came to be.

4 Servings

1 recipe Cornmeal Pasta
4 slices of bacon, diced
1 medium onion, chopped
4 garlic cloves, crushed through a press
1 pound young turnip or mustard greens, trimmed and torn, or 1 (10-ounce) package frozen turnip greens, thawed and well drained

⅔ cup chicken broth
⅔ cup dry white wine
⅔ cup heavy cream
½ to 1 teaspoon Tabasco sauce, to taste
Salt and freshly ground pepper

1. Cut the pasta into ziti or other similar short tubular pasta shape. Let dry on wax paper for at least 15 minutes before using.

2. In a large skillet, cook the bacon over medium heat, stirring often, until crisp, about 5 minutes. Remove with a slotted spoon and drain on paper towels. Add the onion to the drippings in the pan and cook, stirring often, until softened, 3 to 5 minutes. Add the garlic and cook, stirring, for 1 minute. Add the greens and cook, stirring often, until the greens are tender, about 3 minutes. Stir in the broth, wine, and cream. Simmer, stirring often, for 3 minutes. Season with Tabasco and salt and pepper to taste.

3. Cook the ziti in a large pot of boiling salted water until tender but still firm, 4 to 5 minutes. Drain in a colander. Toss the pasta with the sauce and serve.

Dried Herb Pasta

Dried herbs have more potency than fresh, so a small amount goes a long way in pasta dough. For best flavor, start with a newly opened jar or one that you have had on the shelf no longer than a month. Nearly any herb will do, though our favorites are tarragon, marjoram, oregano, thyme, and sage.

Makes 1 pound; recommended for all pasta shapes

---

3 cups all-purpose bleached or unbleached
    flour
1 tablespoon dried herb of choice
½ teaspoon salt

3 "large" eggs
2 teaspoons olive or vegetable oil
Water

---

1. Measure the flour by scooping it into a measuring cup and leveling it off with the back of a knife. Sift it into the mixing container of the pasta machine along with the herb and salt.

2. Break the eggs into a liquid measuring cup. Add the oil and enough water to measure ¾ cup. Use a fork or small whisk to lightly beat the eggs.

3. Start the machine and slowly pour the liquid into the mixing container. Process, adding additional water by tablespoons if needed, and extrude as directed in the machine's manual.

4. Spread the pasta out on wax paper or kitchen towels. Let dry for at least 15 minutes or for up to 2 hours before using. The pasta can be stored in the refrigerator for up to 24 hours or frozen for up to 1 month.

Dill Spaghettini with Scallops and Citrus

Pasta flavored with dill is a lovely companion to scallops and citrus, but tarragon and thyme are good herb choices, too. Scallions and asparagus give this verdant pasta a springtime theme.

4 Servings

---

1 recipe Dried Herb Pasta, made with dill
1 cup dry white wine
½ cup clam juice
1 large garlic clove, peeled and lightly mashed with the flat side of a knife
¾ pound bay or small sea scallops
1 cup light cream

1 teaspoon grated orange zest
½ teaspoon grated lemon zest
½ teaspoon freshly ground pepper
6 ounces snow peas, cut in half on the diagonal
⅓ cup thinly sliced scallions
½ cup shredded Gruyère cheese

---

1. Cut the pasta into spaghettini or thin spaghetti. Let dry on wax paper for at least 15 minutes before using.

2. In a nonreactive medium saucepan, bring the wine, clam juice, and garlic to a simmer. Add the scallops and simmer gently over medium-low heat until the scallops are opaque throughout, 2 to 3 minutes. Use a slotted spoon to remove the scallops from the wine. Raise the heat to medium-high and boil until the liquid is reduced by half. Add the cream, orange zest, lemon zest, and pepper. Reduce the heat to medium and cook until slightly thickened, about 5 minutes. Remove and discard the garlic.

3. Cook the spaghettini in a large pot of boiling salted water until tender but still firm, about 2 minutes. Add the snow peas to the cooking pot during the last 30 seconds. Drain the pasta and snow peas in a colander.

4. Toss the hot pasta with the scallops, sauce, and scallions. Sprinkle the cheese on top and serve.

Pumpkin-Filled Sage Ravioli

If you've never tasted handmade ravioli, you're in for a real treat. Though the process is a bit involved, the labor is satisfying, and the results are well worth the effort. For this recipe, tender egg pasta flavored with sage encloses a smooth pumpkin filling. Pumpkin is traditionally used in some regions of Italy and has also become a favorite in stylish American restaurants.

4 Servings (about 24 large ravioli)

---

1 recipe Dried Herb Pasta, made with sage
All-purpose flour
1 cup canned solid-pack pumpkin
1 egg yolk
½ cup grated Parmesan cheese, plus additional for sprinkling
3 tablespoons fine dry bread crumbs

½ teaspoon salt
½ teaspoon freshly ground pepper
¼ teaspoon grated nutmeg
2 cups reduced-sodium chicken broth
1 teaspoon crumbled dried leaf sage
2 tablespoons butter

---

1. Cut the pasta into lasagne noodles about 7 inches long. Sprinkle lightly with flour and use a rolling pin or hand-cranked pasta machine to make thin sheets about 3 inches wide and 10 inches long. You should have about 16 sheets. Save any remaining pasta for another use. Use immediately or dust lightly with flour, wrap in plastic, and refrigerate up to 2 days or freeze for up to 1 month. Defrost in the refrigerator.

2. In a mixing bowl, whisk the pumpkin with the egg yolk, Parmesan cheese, bread crumbs, salt, pepper, and nutmeg until smooth.

3. Place a pasta sheet on a work surface. Spoon 3 evenly spaced mounds of pumpkin filling on the pasta sheet, using about 2 teaspoons for each mound. Dip a pastry brush in water and moisten the dough around each mound of filling. Cover with another pasta sheet and press gently between the mounds to seal. Use a knife or fluted pastry wheel to cut the ravioli apart into 3-inch squares. Press the edges together to seal well. Repeat with the remaining dough and filling. Let the ravioli dry on a rack or refrigerate for up to 24 hours. To freeze, place on a baking sheet, freeze until firm, and then store in a plastic bag in the freezer.

4. In a medium saucepan, boil the chicken broth with the sage over medium-high heat until the liquid is reduced to about 1 cup. Whisk in the butter.

5. Cook the ravioli in a large pot of boiling salted water until tender but still firm, about 5 minutes. Drain in a colander. Serve the ravioli in wide shallow soup bowls or on rimmed plates with the sauce spooned on top. Pass additional Parmesan cheese at the table.

Herbed Penne with Vodka Sauce

This classic pink, vodka-spiked sauce is wonderful with any herbed pasta. The commercial blend of oregano, marjoram, thyme, savory, sage, oregano, and basil that is called Italian seasoning works particularly well here.

4 Servings

1 recipe Dried Herb Pasta, made with Italian seasoning blend
2 tablespoons extra-virgin olive oil
1 small onion, chopped
2 garlic cloves, crushed through a press
1 cup heavy or light cream
½ cup vodka

¼ cup tomato paste
½ teaspoon crushed hot pepper flakes
1 (14½-ounce) can diced tomatoes, with their juices
¼ cup chopped flat-leaf parsley
Salt

1. Cut the pasta into penne or other similar tubular shape. Let dry on wax paper for at least 15 minutes before using.

2. In a medium skillet, heat the oil. Add the onion and cook over medium heat, stirring often, until softened, 3 to 5 minutes. Add the garlic and cook 1 minute. Add the cream, vodka, tomato paste, hot pepper, and tomatoes. Simmer, stirring often, until slightly reduced, about 10 minutes.

3. Cook the penne in a large pot of boiling salted water until tender but still firm, 3 to 5 minutes. Drain in a colander. Toss the pasta with the sauce. Add the parsley and salt to taste, toss again, and serve.

Veal Saltimbocca over Sage Linguine

4 Servings

1 recipe Dried Herb Pasta, made with sage
¾ pound veal scallops, cut from the leg
Salt and freshly ground pepper
3 tablespoons butter
2 ounces thinly sliced prosciutto
3 ounces thinly sliced or grated Italian
    fontina or Edam cheese

¼ cup finely chopped shallots
½ teaspoon grated lemon zest
¾ cup dry white wine
¾ cup chicken broth

1. Cut the pasta into linguine. Let dry on wax paper for at least 15 minutes before using. Preheat the oven to 300 degrees.

2. Season the veal with salt and pepper. Melt the butter in a large skillet over medium-high heat. Add the veal and cook for 2 minutes. Turn the veal over and top with the prosciutto and cheese. Reduce the heat to medium and cover the pan. Cook until the cheese is melted and the veal is cooked through, about 2 minutes.

3. Remove the veal from the pan and keep warm on a baking sheet or ovenproof platter in the preheated oven. Add the shallots to the pan drippings and cook until softened, 1 or 2 minutes. Add the lemon zest, wine, and broth. Raise the heat to medium-high and bring to a boil, stirring up the browned bits clinging to the bottom of the pan. Boil until slightly reduced, about 3 minutes.

4. Meanwhile, cook the linguine in a large pot of boiling salted water until tender but still firm, about 2 minutes. Drain in a colander. Toss the pasta with the sauce. Divide the pasta among 4 serving plates and top with the veal.

Crab-Filled Tarragon Tortellini

Good tortellini—both fresh and frozen—are now readily available, but when you make your own flavored pasta doughs, these lovely little pasta rings can be custom-made to your taste. We love this juxtaposition of delicate tarragon-flecked dough and sweet crab filling, but you can have lots of fun coming up with your own compatible flavor combinations.

4 Servings (about 48 tortellini)

1 recipe Dried Herb Pasta, made with tarragon	2 teaspoons lemon juice
All-purpose flour	¼ teaspoon salt
6 ounces cream cheese, softened	¼ teaspoon cayenne
2 tablespoons fine dry bread crumbs	1 (16-ounce) can stewed tomatoes
3 tablespoons minced scallions	¾ cup dry white wine
	1 tablespoon butter

1. Cut the pasta into lasagne noodles about 7 inches long. Sprinkle lightly with flour and use a rolling pin or hand-cranked pasta machine to make sheets about 3 inches wide and 10 inches long. You should have about 16 sheets. Save any remaining dough for another use. Use immediately or dust lightly with flour, wrap in plastic, and refrigerate up to 2 days or freeze. Defrost in the refrigerator.

2. In a mixing bowl, stir together the crabmeat, cream cheese, and bread crumbs until smooth. Stir in the scallions, lemon juice, salt, and cayenne.

3. Use a 3-inch cookie cutter to cut 3 rounds out of each sheet of pasta. Spoon about 1 teaspoon of crab filling into the center of each round. Brush the edges with water to moisten. Fold over to make a half-circle and press the edges to seal. Bring the 2 pointed ends together and pinch to seal. Let dry on a rack for 30 minutes or refrigerate for up to 24 hours. To freeze, place the tortellini on a baking sheet, freeze until firm, and then store in a plastic bag in the freezer.

4. In a medium nonreactive saucepan, combine the stewed tomatoes and wine, breaking up the tomatoes with the side of a spoon into smaller chunks. Simmer, uncovered, over medium heat until somewhat reduced and thickened, about 10 minutes. Whisk in the butter. Reheat if necessary before using.

5. Cook the tortellini in a large pot of rapidly boiling salted water until tender but still firm, 3 to 4 minutes. Drain in a colander. Serve the tortellini in wide shallow soup bowls or on rimmed plates with the sauce spooned over the pasta.

Tarragon Capellini Primavera

Primavera, which translates literally into "first of spring," is often interpreted to mean a pasta with any vegetable at all. This rendition is true to the name, using only the most delicate of spring vegetables.

4 Servings

---

1 recipe Dried Herb Pasta, made with tarragon
2 tablespoons butter
2 slender leeks (white part only), thinly sliced
¼ pound baby carrots
¼ pound slender asparagus, trimmed and cut into 1-inch diagonal lengths
½ cup frozen baby green peas

1 cup light cream
⅔ cup chicken broth
1 tablespoon lemon juice
½ teaspoon grated lemon zest
⅓ cup minced chives
¼ cup thinly sliced small radishes
⅓ cup grated Parmesan cheese
½ teaspoon freshly ground white pepper

---

1. Cut the pasta into capellini or vermicelli. Let dry on wax paper for at least 15 minutes before using.

2. In a large skillet, melt the butter over medium heat. Add the leeks and carrots and cook, stirring often, until the carrots are beginning to soften, about 5 minutes. Add the asparagus, peas, cream, broth, lemon juice, and lemon zest. Cook, stirring often, until the asparagus is crisp-tender and the cream is slightly reduced, about 3 minutes. Stir in the chives.

3. Meanwhile, cook the capellini in a large pot of boiling salted water until tender but still firm, 3 to 5 minutes. Drain in a colander. Toss the pasta with the sauce. Add the radishes, cheese, and pepper. Toss again and serve.

Jalapeño Pasta

There are just enough jalapeño peppers here to give the pasta a bit of a kick but not so many that they overwhelm a sauce. This pasta is especially good in tandem with other spicy ingredients, but we like it simply tossed with a little oil and broth and some fresh herbs, too.

Makes 1 pound; use for spaghetti, linguine, tubular macaroni, lasagne

---

3 cups all-purpose bleached or unbleached
    flour
½ teaspoon salt
3 "large" eggs

1 tablespoon minced fresh or pickled jala-
    peño peppers
2 teaspoons olive or vegetable oil
Water

---

1. Measure the flour by scooping it into a measuring cup and leveling it off with the back of a knife. Sift it into the mixing container of the pasta machine along with the salt.
2. Break the eggs into a liquid measuring cup. Add the jalapeños, oil, and enough water to make ¾ cup. Use a fork or small whisk to lightly beat the eggs.
3. Start the machine and slowly pour the liquid into the mixing container. Process, adding additional water by tablespoons, and extrude as directed in the machine's manual.
4. Spread the pasta out on wax paper or kitchen towels. Let dry for at least 15 minutes or for up to 2 hours before using. The pasta can be stored in the refrigerator for up to 24 hours or frozen for up to 1 month.

Jalapeño Penne with Turkey Mole Sauce

Mole is a classic long-simmered Mexican sauce that includes many herbs, spices, nuts, seeds, and even some chocolate. It is traditionally served over braised turkey. This quick and easy version features boneless fillets of turkey.

4 Servings

---

1 recipe Jalapeño Pasta

2 tablespoons sesame seeds

1 pound skinless, boneless turkey breast fillets or paillards

Salt and freshly ground pepper

3 tablespoons vegetable oil

1 medium onion, chopped

1 large garlic clove, crushed through a press

1 tablespoon chili powder

½ teaspoon ground cumin

½ teaspoon dried oregano

¼ teaspoon ground coriander

¼ teaspoon ground cinnamon

1 (14½-ounce) can Mexican- or salsa-style stewed tomatoes

1 cup chicken broth

½ ounce (½ square) unsweetened chocolate, chopped

1 tablespoon chopped cilantro

---

1. Cut the pasta into penne or other short tubular shape. Let dry on wax paper for at least 15 minutes before using. Toast the sesame seeds by stirring them in a small skillet over medium heat until golden and fragrant, about 3 minutes. Remove the skillet immediately to prevent burning.

2. Season the turkey lightly with salt and pepper. In a large skillet, heat 2 tablespoons of the oil. Add the turkey and cook over medium-high heat, turning once, until golden, about 3 minutes. Remove the turkey from the skillet. Add the remaining 1 tablespoon of oil to the skillet. Reduce the heat to medium, add the onion, and cook, stirring often, until softened, 3 to 5 minutes. Add the garlic and chili powder and cook for 1 minute.

Stir in the cumin, oregano, coriander, cinnamon, tomatoes, broth, and 1 tablespoon of the sesame seeds. Bring to a boil, reduce the heat to medium-low, and simmer until slightly thickened, about 15 minutes. Stir in the chocolate until melted. Return the turkey to the skillet and simmer for 5 minutes. Stir in the cilantro.

3. Cook the penne in a large pot of boiling salted water until tender but still firm, 3 to 5 minutes. Toss the pasta with the sauce. Sprinkle with the remaining sesame seeds and serve.

Fast and Fabulous Jalapeño Noodle Tuna Tetrazzini

4 Servings

1 recipe Jalapeño Pasta
2 (6-ounce) cans tuna packed in oil, preferably olive oil
1 medium onion, coarsely chopped
1 small red bell pepper, coarsely chopped
1 small yellow bell pepper, coarsely chopped
2 garlic cloves, crushed through a press

1 tablespoon chili powder
1 teaspoon ground cumin
2 cups half-and-half or light cream
½ cup clam juice
½ cup dry white wine
½ cup grated Parmesan cheese
¼ cup plain dry bread crumbs

1. Cut the pasta into noodles or fettuccine. Let dry on wax paper for at least 15 minutes before using. Preheat the broiler.

2. Drain ¼ cup of the oil from the tuna into a large ovenproof skillet. Heat the oil and add the onion and both bell peppers. Cook over medium heat, stirring often, until the vegetables are tender, about 5 minutes. Add the garlic, chili powder, and cumin and cook, stirring, for 30 seconds. Stir in the cream, clam juice, and wine. Bring to a boil, reduce the heat to medium-low, and simmer until slightly thickened, about 5 minutes.

3. Cook the noodles in a large pot of boiling salted water until tender but still firm, 2 to 3 minutes. Drain in a colander.

4. Add the noodles to the sauce in the skillet along with half of the cheese. Toss to blend. Combine the remaining cheese with the bread crumbs and sprinkle on top of the noodles. Broil about 4 inches from the heat until the crumbs are browned and crisp, about 2 minutes. (If the casserole is assembled ahead of time, sprinkle with the cheese and crumbs and bake in a preheated 375 degree oven until heated through and the crumbs are crisp and brown, 20 to 25 minutes.)

Jalapeño Rigatoni with Pico de Gallo and Jack Cheese Salsa

In summer, we love uncooked tomato sauces for pasta. They are quick, easy, and really take advantage of the unequaled taste of garden fresh tomatoes. If you make this with regular pasta, use Monterey Jack cheese with jalapeño peppers.

1 recipe Jalapeño Pasta
1½ pounds ripe meaty tomatoes
1 small green bell pepper, coarsely chopped
½ small jicama, peeled and coarsely chopped (about ¾ cup)
6 tablespoons extra-virgin olive oil

2 tablespoons red wine vinegar
1 teaspoon salt
2 garlic cloves, crushed through a press
6 ounces Monterey Jack cheese, finely diced
¼ cup chopped cilantro

1. Cut the pasta into rigatoni or other similar short shape. Let dry on wax paper for at least 15 minutes before using.

2. Bring a large pot of salted water to a boil. Plunge the tomatoes into the water for 20 seconds and then remove from the water. Leave the water boiling. Peel, seed, and coarsely chop the tomatoes. Place in a mixing bowl along with the bell pepper, jicama, oil, vinegar, salt, garlic, cheese, and cilantro.

3. Cook the rigatoni in the boiling salted water until tender but still firm, 3 to 5 minutes. Drain in a colander. Return the pasta to the hot cooking pot. Add the salsa. Toss until the cheese is partially melted, about 1 minute. Serve at once.

Jalapeño Spaghetti Pie

Jalapeño-flavored spaghetti is cooked, tossed with egg and milk, and spread out to form a "pie crust" base for the savory topping made with ground pork, kidney beans, and our favorite Tex-Mex seasonings. This is a scrumptious make-ahead casserole—perfect for a family or company dinner.

8 Servings

---

1 recipe Jalapeño Pasta	1½ teaspoons dried oregano
2 eggs	2 (16-ounce) cans tomato sauce
¾ cup milk	1 (14- to 16-ounce) can kidney beans,
1 pound ground pork	rinsed and drained
1 large onion, chopped	½ teaspoon salt
1 green bell pepper, chopped	½ teaspoon freshly ground black pepper
2 tablespoons chili powder	¼ teaspoon cayenne
1½ teaspoons ground cumin	3 cups shredded Monterey Jack cheese

---

1. Cut the pasta into spaghetti. Let dry on wax paper for at least 15 minutes before using. Cook the spaghetti in a large pot of boiling salted water until tender but still firm, 2 to 3 minutes. Drain in a colander.

2. In a large bowl, whisk the eggs with the milk. Add the spaghetti, toss to combine, and spread evenly in a greased shallow, 3-quart baking dish.

3. In a large skillet, cook the pork with the onion and bell pepper over medium-high heat, stirring frequently, until the meat loses its pink color, about 8 minutes. Add the chili powder, cumin, and oregano and cook, stirring, for 1 minute. Add the tomato sauce and beans and simmer, uncovered, over medium heat for about 15 minutes to blend the flavors. Season with the salt, black pepper, and cayenne.

4. Spoon the meat sauce over the spaghetti and sprinkle evenly with the cheese. Cover with foil. If not baking immediately, refrigerate for up to 6 hours. Return to room temperature before baking.

5. Preheat the oven to 350 degrees. Bake the casserole, covered, for 30 minutes. Uncover and cook until the casserole is heated through and the cheese melts, 15 to 20 minutes.

Sloppy Joe Jalapeño Spaghetti

4 Servings

---

1 pound lean ground chuck
1 medium onion, chopped
1 green bell pepper, chopped
2 garlic cloves, crushed through a press
1 tablespoon chili powder
2 (14½-ounce) cans diced tomatoes
1 cup beef broth
½ cup bottled chili sauce
1 tablespoon red wine vinegar

2 teaspoons light brown sugar
2 teaspoons Worcestershire sauce
¼ cup chopped fresh parsley
1½ teaspoons dried basil
¾ teaspoon dried thyme
¾ teaspoon dried marjoram
Salt and freshly ground pepper
1 recipe Jalapeño Pasta

---

1. In a large skillet, cook the beef over medium heat, stirring often, until it begins to lose its red color, about 5 minutes. Add the onion, bell pepper, and garlic. Cook, stirring often, until the vegetables begin to soften, about 5 minutes. Pour off any excess fat.

2. Stir in the chili powder and cook for 30 seconds. Add the tomatoes, broth, chili sauce, vinegar, brown sugar, Worcestershire sauce, parsley, basil, thyme, and marjoram. Season to taste with salt and pepper. Reduce the heat to medium-low and simmer for 20 minutes. Use immediately or refrigerate for up to 3 days. Reheat at serving time.

3. Cut the pasta into spaghetti. Let dry on wax paper for at least 15 minutes before using. Cook the spaghetti in a large pot of boiling salted water until tender but still firm, 2 to 3 minutes. Drain in a colander. Ladle the meat sauce over the spaghetti and serve.

Lemon Pasta

Tart in flavor and light in texture, this is a perfect pasta to pair with spring vegetables and seafood of all kinds.

Makes 1 pound; recommended for all pasta shapes

---

3 cups all-purpose bleached or unbleached
    flour
½ teaspoon salt
2 "large" eggs

2 tablespoons lemon juice
2 teaspoons vegetable oil
2 teaspoons finely grated lemon zest
Water

---

1. Measure the flour by scooping it into a measuring cup and leveling it off with the back of a knife. Sift it into the mixing container of the pasta machine along with the salt.
2. Break the eggs into a liquid measuring cup. Add the lemon juice, oil, zest, and enough water to measure ¾ cup. Use a fork or small whisk to lightly beat the eggs.
3. Start the machine and slowly pour the liquid into the mixing container. Process, adding additional water by tablespoons if needed, and extrude as directed in the machine's manual.
4. Spread the pasta out on wax paper or kitchen towels. Let dry for at least 15 minutes or for up to 2 hours before using. The pasta can be stored in the refrigerator for up to 24 hours or frozen for up to 1 month.

Lemon Angel Hair Bagna Cauda

The classic Italian bagna cauda, *literally "warm bath," is a blend of oil and butter simmered with garlic and mashed anchovies. We added lemon, both in the sauce and in the pasta, to add fresh sparkle.*

4 Servings

---

1 pound Lemon Pasta
¼ cup olive oil
1½ tablespoons unsalted butter
5 anchovy fillets
3 large garlic cloves, crushed through a
    press

½ cup chicken broth
¼ cup lemon juice
1 teaspoon grated lemon zest
⅓ cup chopped flat-leaf parsley
½ teaspoon freshly ground pepper

---

1. Cut the pasta into angel hair or capellini. Let dry on wax paper for at least 15 minutes before using.

2. In a small saucepan, cook the oil, butter, anchovies, and garlic over medium-low heat, stirring and mashing the anchovies with the back of a spoon until the mixture comes to a simmer and they dissolve. Simmer gently for 3 minutes. Stir in the broth, lemon juice, and lemon zest. Simmer for 2 minutes.

3. Meanwhile, cook the angel hair pasta in a large pot of boiling salted water until tender but still firm, about 1 minute. Drain in a colander. Toss the pasta with the sauce. Add the parsley and pepper, toss again, and serve at once.

Lemon Bow Ties with Country Ham
and Dilled Green Peas

If your machine has a ruffled edge noodle cutter, you can make bow ties by cutting 2-inch lengths, then firmly pinching the pieces together in the middle to form bow ties. Let the pasta dry for at least 2 hours before using so that the bows will retain their shape during cooking.

4 Servings

---

1 recipe Lemon Pasta

3 ounces cooked country ham or well-flavored smoked ham, diced (about 1 cup)

2 tablespoons butter

⅔ cup thinly sliced scallions

1 large garlic clove, crushed through a press

1 cup heavy cream

¾ cup dry white wine

½ cup chicken broth

¾ cup frozen tiny green peas, thawed

2 tablespoons chopped fresh dill or 2 teaspoons dried

½ teaspoon freshly ground pepper

Fresh dill sprigs (optional)

---

1. Cut the pasta into bow ties or a short tubular shape. Let the bow ties dry on wax paper for at least 2 hours before using.

2. In a medium skillet, cook the ham in the butter over medium-high heat, stirring constantly, until the ham is golden, about 4 minutes. Add the scallions and garlic, reduce the heat to medium, and cook, stirring often, for 2 minutes. Add the cream, wine, and broth. Boil until slightly thickened, about 3 minutes. Add the peas, chopped dill, and pepper. Simmer for 2 minutes.

3. Cook the bow ties in a large pot of boiling salted water until tender but still firm, 3 to 4 minutes; drain. Toss the bow ties with the sauce. Garnish with dill sprigs.

Seafood Lasagne with Lemon Pasta

8 Servings

1 recipe Lemon Pasta
3 tablespoons olive oil
1 large onion, chopped
1½ cups thinly sliced fennel (about
  1 bulb)
3 garlic cloves, crushed through a press
2 (28-ounce) cans plum tomatoes, drained
  and coarsely chopped
¾ cup clam juice
¾ cup dry white wine
½ cup slivered oil-packed sun-dried
  tomatoes

½ teaspoon crushed hot pepper flakes
1 pound monkfish or other firm-fleshed
  white fish, cut into 1-inch chunks
¾ pound medium shrimp, shelled and
  deveined
½ pound cleaned squid, thinly sliced into
  rings
½ cup chopped parsley
2 tablespoons anise-flavored liqueur, such
  as Pernod
Salt
⅓ cup grated Parmesan cheese

1. Cut the pasta into lasagne noodles about 6 inches long. Use a rolling pin or hand-cranked pasta machine to roll out to a thickness of about 1/16 inch. Cook the lasagne noodles in a large pot of boiling salted water until tender but still firm, 1 to 2 minutes. Drain in a colander.

2. In a large skillet, heat the oil over medium heat. Add the onion and fennel and cook, stirring frequently, until softened, about 5 minutes. Add the garlic and cook until fragrant, 1 minute. Add the tomatoes, clam juice, wine, sun-dried tomatoes, and hot pepper. Cook, uncovered, stirring occasionally, until most of the liquid evaporates, 10 to 15 minutes. Add the monkfish, shrimp, and squid and simmer until the seafood is cooked through, about 5 minutes. Stir in the parsley and anise liqueur. Taste and season with salt if necessary.

3. Oil 8 individual gratin dishes or a shallow 3- to 4-quart baking dish. Use one-third of the lasagne noodles to make a layer in the bottom of the dish(es), trimming to fit if necessary. Spoon one-third of the sauce over the pasta. Repeat the layering two more times, ending with pasta and topping with sauce. Sprinkle with the Parmesan cheese. If not baking immediately, refrigerate for up to 6 hours. Return to room temperature before baking.

4. Preheat the oven to 400 degrees. Bake the lasagne, uncovered, in the preheated oven until the cheese is lightly glazed, the sauce is bubbly, and the noodles begin to crisp around the edges, 15 to 20 minutes.

Lemon Noodles Osso Buco

Osso buco is a classic Italian stew made with long-simmered veal shanks. We've developed a streamlined version with boneless veal shoulder, which takes only about 30 minutes to make. But it is the last-minute sprinkling of gremolata, a mix of fresh chopped parsley, lemon zest, and garlic, that really makes the dish.

4 to 6 Servings

1 recipe Lemon Pasta
¼ cup all-purpose flour
½ teaspoon salt
¼ teaspoon freshly ground pepper
1 pound boneless veal shoulder, cut into
   1-inch chunks
¼ cup olive oil
1 medium onion, coarsely chopped
2 slender carrots, peeled and coarsely
   chopped

1 celery rib, coarsely chopped
1½ cups chicken broth
½ cup dry white wine
1 bay leaf, broken in half
⅓ cup chopped flat-leaf parsley
2 teaspoons grated lemon zest
2 garlic cloves, minced

1. Cut the pasta into medium noodles. Let dry on wax paper for at least 15 minutes before using.

2. In a plastic bag, shake together the flour, salt, and pepper. Add the veal in batches and shake to coat with the seasoned flour. In a large skillet, heat 2 tablespoons of the oil over medium-high heat. Add the veal and cook, turning, until all sides are golden, 5 to 7 minutes. Remove the meat to a plate.

3. Add the remaining 2 tablespoons of oil to the pan, reduce the heat to medium, and cook the onion, carrots, and celery, stirring often, until the vegetables are softened, about

5 minutes. Return the meat to the pan, add the broth, wine, and bay leaf, and bring to a simmer. Reduce the heat to medium-low, cover, and cook for 20 minutes.

4. While the meat is cooking, combine the parsley, lemon zest, and garlic in a small dish. Add half of this gremolata to the sauce and simmer 5 minutes. Remove and discard the bay leaf. Season to taste with salt and pepper.

5. Cook the noodles in a large pot of boiling salted water until tender but still firm, 2 to 3 minutes. Drain in a colander. Toss the noodles with the sauce. Sprinkle with the remaining gremolata and serve.

Lemon Spaghettini with Smoked Salmon and Capers

4 Servings

---

1 recipe Lemon Pasta
2 tablespoons butter
2 tablespoons extra-virgin olive oil
¼ cup chopped shallots
1 cup heavy cream
¾ cup dry white wine
⅓ cup chicken broth

1 tablespoon chopped fresh tarragon or
 ¾ teaspoon dried
¼ pound small snow peas, trimmed
¾ teaspoon coarsely ground pepper
6 ounces thinly sliced smoked salmon, cut
 into ¼-inch-wide strips
2 tablespoons drained small capers

---

1. Cut the pasta into spaghettini or thin spaghetti. Let dry on wax paper for at least 15 minutes before using.

2. In a medium skillet, melt the butter in the oil. Add the shallots and cook over medium heat, stirring, until softened, about 2 minutes. Add the cream, wine, broth, and tarragon and bring to a boil. Reduce the heat to medium-low and simmer until slightly thickened, about 3 minutes.

3. Cook the spaghettini in a large pot of boiling salted water until tender but still firm, 1 to 2 minutes. Add the snow peas to the spaghettini in the pot during the last 30 seconds of cooking. Drain the pasta and snow peas in a colander.

4. Toss the spaghettini with the snow peas, sauce, pepper, and half each of the smoked salmon and capers. Spoon onto a serving platter and sprinkle the remaining smoked salmon and capers over the top.

Pasta Neri (Black Pasta with Squid Ink)

The distinctive, nearly black color of this pasta comes from the "ink" of the Mediterranean cuttlefish. Sold in cans, it is also known as squid ink or seppie. Though canned cuttlefish ink is available at many Italian and Latin American markets, you might have a hard time finding it. Nonetheless, this pasta is so interesting that we decided to include the recipe anyway.

The "ink" has an illustrious history and was the medium used by the sepia paintings of the great masters. It also imparts a light and pleasant flavor of the sea to pasta, risottos, and sauces that are often termed "neri," after the brilliant purple-black color of the ink. (It also stains your hands, so be forewarned!) If you can't find cuttlefish "ink," make the following three recipes with Semolina Pasta or Lemon Pasta.

Makes 1 pound; recommended for all pasta shapes, but especially spaghetti

---

3 cups all-purpose bleached or unbleached
    flour
2 "large" eggs

¼ cup cuttlefish ink
Water

---

1. Measure the flour by scooping it into a measuring cup and leveling it off with the back of a knife. Sift it into the mixing container of the pasta machine.

2. Break the eggs into a liquid measuring cup. Add the cuttlefish ink and enough water to make ¾ cup. Use a fork or small whisk to lightly beat the eggs.

3. Start the machine and slowly pour the liquid into the mixing container. Process, adding additional water by tablespoons if needed, and extrude as directed in the machine's manual.

4. Spread the pasta out on wax paper or kitchen towels. Let dry for at least 15 minutes or for up to 2 hours before using. The pasta can be stored in the refrigerator up to 24 hours or frozen for up to 1 month.

Capellini Neri with Shrimp and Toasted Bread Crumbs

4 Servings

---

1 recipe Pasta Neri

3 or 4 slices of day-old Italian bread, torn into pieces

5 tablespoons extra-virgin olive oil

3 large garlic cloves, crushed through a press

¾ cup dry white wine

¾ cup clam juice

¼ teaspoon crushed hot pepper flakes

¾ pound medium shrimp, shelled and deveined

1 tablespoon chopped fresh marjoram or 1 teaspoon dried

1 cup chopped flat-leaf parsley

⅓ cup grated Pecorino Romano cheese

---

1. Cut the pasta into capellini. Let dry on wax paper for at least 15 minutes before using. Process the bread in a food processor to make about 1 cup crumbs.

2. In a large skillet, heat 1 tablespoon of the oil. Add the bread crumbs and cook over medium-high heat, stirring constantly, until golden and crisp, 3 to 4 minutes. Remove the bread crumbs to a small bowl, but do not wipe out the skillet.

3. Add the remaining ¼ cup oil to the skillet and cook the garlic over medium-low heat until softened, about 1 minute. Add the wine, clam juice, and hot pepper. Raise the heat to medium and boil until slightly reduced, 3 to 4 minutes. Add the shrimp and marjoram and cook until the shrimp are pink and curled, about 3 minutes. Add the parsley.

4. Cook the capellini in a large pot of boiling salted water until tender but still firm, about 1 minute. Drain in a colander. Toss the capellini with the sauce and spoon onto a large platter. Combine the cheese and the bread crumbs and sprinkle over the pasta.

Linguine Neri with Seafood Romesco Sauce

4 Servings

6 tablespoons slivered almonds
2 large garlic cloves, coarsely chopped
1 (7-ounce) jar roasted peppers, drained,
  with liquid reserved
1 (3½-ounce) can chopped green chiles,
  drained
1 large tomato, peeled and seeded, or
  3 drained canned plum tomatoes
1 slice of French bread, cut 1 inch thick,
  toasted and torn into pieces

¼ teaspoon cayenne
¼ cup dry red or white wine
1 tablespoon sherry wine vinegar
¼ cup olive oil
1 recipe Pasta Neri
1 recipe Grilled Seafood Brochettes (recipe
  follows)

1. In a small frying pan set over medium heat, stir the almonds until they are golden brown and fragrant, about 3 minutes. Remove immediately from the pan to prevent burning. Place the almonds, garlic, roasted peppers, chiles, tomato, bread, cayenne, wine, and vinegar in a food processor. Process, scraping down the sides once or twice, until all ingredients are finely chopped. With the machine on, pour the oil through the feed tube, processing until coarsely pureed. The sauce should be thick but pourable. If it is too thick, add enough reserved roasted pepper liquid to thin slightly. Use the Romesco Sauce immediately or refrigerate for up to 2 days, but reheat before serving.

2. Cut the pasta into linguine. Let dry on wax paper for at least 15 minutes before using. Cook the linguine in a large pot of boiling salted water until tender but still firm, about 2 minutes. Drain in a colander.

3. Transfer the linguine to a large platter or 4 serving plates. Ladle the Romesco Sauce over the pasta. Top with Grilled Seafood Brochettes and serve at once.

Grilled Seafood Brochettes

Vary these brochettes by using other seafood combinations, such as salmon or monkfish and large sea scallops. They are delicious over Pasta Neri but are also wonderful with Scallion Pasta, Basil and Garlic Pasta, or Dried Herb Pasta.

4 Servings

---

2 tablespoons olive oil
2 tablespoons lemon juice
2 tablespoons chopped fresh basil
½ teaspoon salt
¼ teaspoon freshly ground pepper
⅓ pound swordfish steak, cut into 1-inch chunks

⅓ pound tuna steak, cut into 1-inch chunks
⅓ pound extra-large shrimp, shelled and deveined

---

1. In a shallow dish just large enough to hold the seafood, combine the oil, lemon juice, basil, salt, and pepper. Add the swordfish, tuna, and shrimp and turn to coat all over. Let stand at room temperature for up to 30 minutes or refrigerate for up to 1 hour.
2. Prepare a hot barbecue fire or preheat a gas grill. Thread the seafood, alternating types, onto 4 metal skewers. Grill, turning occasionally, until browned outside and just opaque in the center, about 8 minutes.

Spaghetti Neri with Peppery Calamari Sauce

Buy fresh calamari, aka squid, from a reputable seafood market, where they will clean it for you. Don't overcook squid, as it quickly becomes tough.

4 Servings

---

1 recipe Pasta Neri
1 medium onion, chopped
2 tablespoons olive oil
3 garlic cloves, crushed through a press
1 teaspoon dried oregano
½ teaspoon crushed hot pepper flakes
2 (14½-ounce) cans Italian-style stewed
   tomatoes

½ cup dry red wine
1 pound fresh calamari, or squid, cleaned,
   bodies sliced into rings
½ cup chopped flat-leaf parsley
¼ cup chopped fresh basil
¼ cup grated Parmesan cheese

---

1. Cut the pasta into spaghetti. Let dry on wax paper for at least 15 minutes before using.
2. In a large skillet, cook the onion in the oil over medium heat, stirring often, until softened, about 5 minutes. Add the garlic and cook for 1 minute. Add the oregano, hot pepper, tomatoes, and wine. Cook until slightly reduced, about 5 minutes. Add the calamari and cook until tender, 1 to 2 minutes. Stir in the parsley and basil.
3. Meanwhile, cook the spaghetti in a large pot of boiling salted water until tender but still firm, 2 to 3 minutes. Drain in a colander. Toss the spaghetti with the sauce. Sprinkle with the cheese.

Orange Pasta

Orange and tomato are a naturally good flavor combination, so this pasta teams up well with almost any tomato sauce as well as with seafood and vegetable sauces.

Makes 1 pound; recommended for all pasta shapes

---

3 cups all-purpose bleached or unbleached
    flour
½ teaspoon salt
2 "large" eggs

¼ cup orange juice
2 teaspoons finely grated orange zest
Water

---

1. Measure the flour by scooping it into a measuring cup and leveling it off with the back of a knife. Sift it into the mixing container of the pasta machine along with the salt.
2. Break the eggs into a liquid measuring cup. Add the orange juice, zest, and enough water to measure ¾ cup. Use a fork or small whisk to lightly beat the eggs.
3. Start the machine and slowly pour the liquid into the mixing container. Process, adding additional water by tablespoons if needed, and extrude as directed in the machine's manual.
4. Spread the pasta out on wax paper or kitchen towels. Let dry for at least 15 minutes or for up to 2 hours before using. The pasta can be stored in the refrigerator for up to 24 hours or frozen for up to 1 month.

Orange Angel Hair with Sorrel Cream

Sorrel is a distinctive leafy green with a slightly lemony accent and is worth seeking out in both the spring and fall. The sauce can be made with frozen chopped spinach, though the flavor will be quite different.

4 Servings

1 recipe Orange Pasta	½ cup chicken broth
2 tablespoons butter	2 tablespoons lemon juice
¼ cup chopped shallots	1 teaspoon grated lemon zest
1 large bunch of sorrel (about 4 ounces), shredded	¼ teaspoon ground mace
	1 cup heavy cream
½ cup dry white wine	Salt and freshly ground pepper

1. Cut the pasta into angel hair or capellini. Let dry on wax paper for at least 15 minutes before using.

2. In a large skillet, melt the butter. Add the shallots and cook over medium heat, stirring, until softened, 1 to 2 minutes. Stir in the sorrel, wine, broth, lemon juice, lemon zest, and mace. Bring to a simmer, reduce the heat to medium-low, and cook, stirring often, until the sorrel is very soft, 3 to 4 minutes. Add the cream and simmer 2 minutes. Season to taste with salt and pepper.

3. Cook the angel hair in a large pot of boiling salted water until tender but still firm, about 1 minute. Drain in a colander. Toss the pasta with the sauce and serve at once.

Orange Fettuccine and Provençal Fisherman's Sauce

4 Servings

1 recipe Orange Pasta
1 small fennel bulb (about 4 ounces), chopped, with fennel fronds reserved
1 large onion, thinly sliced
3 tablespoons extra-virgin olive oil
3 large garlic cloves, crushed through a press
2 (14½-ounce) cans Italian-style stewed tomatoes
½ cup clam juice

½ cup dry white wine
2 tablespoons Pernod
1 teaspoon dried marjoram
½ teaspoon fennel seeds
¼ teaspoon crushed hot pepper flakes
¾ pound monkfish or other firm fish fillets, cut into 1-inch chunks
8 mussels, scrubbed and debearded
8 clams, scrubbed
8 large shrimp, shelled and deveined

1. Cut the pasta into fettuccine. Let dry on wax paper for at least 15 minutes before using.
2. In a large pot, cook the fennel and onion in the oil over medium heat, stirring often, until the vegetables are softened, about 5 minutes. Add the garlic and cook for 1 minute. Add the tomatoes, clam juice, wine, Pernod, marjoram, fennel seeds, and hot pepper. Partially cover the pot, reduce the heat to medium-low, and simmer for 15 minutes.
3. Add the fish, mussels, clams, and shrimp to the sauce. Simmer until the mussels and clams open and the shrimp are pink and curled, 3 to 5 minutes.
4. Meanwhile, cook the fettuccine in a large pot of boiling salted water until tender but still firm, 2 to 3 minutes. Drain in a colander. Divide the fettuccine among 4 shallow soup dishes. Ladle the seafood and broth over the pasta.

Shrimp Scampi over Orange Linguine

Shrimp and orange go very well together, especially in conjunction with a peppery accent as a counterpoint to the sweetness of the citrus. Here, we use pepper in three ways: crushed hot pepper flakes, black pepper, and a finish with Tabasco sauce. Each lends its own character to the finished dish.

4 Servings

1 recipe Orange Pasta
3 tablespoons extra-virgin olive oil
¼ cup finely chopped shallots
3 large garlic cloves, crushed through a
  press
¾ cup dry white wine
¾ cup clam juice
¼ teaspoon crushed hot pepper flakes

¼ teaspoon freshly ground black pepper
1 tablespoon Worcestershire sauce
1 pound medium or large shrimp, shelled
  and deveined
1 tablespoon Cognac or brandy
½ teaspoon Tabasco sauce
⅓ cup finely chopped flat-leaf parsley

1. Cut the pasta into linguine. Let dry on wax paper for at least 15 minutes before using.
2. In a large skillet, heat the oil. Add the shallots and garlic and cook over medium heat, stirring, for 1 minute. Stir in the wine, clam juice, hot pepper, black pepper, and Worcestershire sauce. Cook for 2 minutes. Add the shrimp, spreading them out to cover the bottom of the pan. Cover and cook until the shrimp just turn pink, about 3 minutes. Stir in the Cognac, Tabasco sauce, and parsley. Cook 1 minute longer.
3. Meanwhile, cook the linguine in a large pot of boiling salted water until tender but still firm, about 2 minutes. Drain in a colander. Toss the linguine with the sauce and serve.

Orange Spaghettini with Mint Pesto

4 Servings

1 cup lightly packed fresh mint leaves

⅔ cup lightly packed fresh flat-leaf parsley sprigs

⅓ cup grated Parmesan cheese

¼ cup pine nuts (pignoli)

3 garlic cloves

1 tablespoon lemon juice

1 tablespoon orange juice

1 teaspoon grated lemon zest

1 teaspoon grated orange zest

¼ teaspoon salt

¼ teaspoon freshly ground pepper

⅓ cup extra-virgin olive oil

1 recipe Orange Pasta

⅔ cup chicken broth

⅔ cup dry white wine

2 ounces thinly sliced prosciutto, cut into thin strips (about ⅓ cup)

1. Place the mint, parsley, cheese, pine nuts, garlic, lemon juice, orange juice, lemon zest, orange zest, salt, and pepper in a food processor. Process, scraping the bowl once or twice, until a coarse puree forms. With the machine on, pour in the olive oil and process until the sauce is pureed, about 10 seconds. Use immediately or cover and refrigerate for up to 24 hours. Return to room temperature before using.

2. Cut the pasta into spaghettini or thin spaghetti. Let dry on wax paper for at least 15 minutes before using.

3. In a small saucepan, boil the broth and wine over medium-high heat until reduced by about one-third, 3 to 4 minutes. Stir in the pesto and remove from the heat.

4. Cook the spaghettini in a large pot of boiling salted water until tender but still firm, about 2 minutes. Drain in a colander. Toss the spaghettini with the sauce and prosciutto and serve.

Potato Gnocchi

Most pasta machines come equipped with a special extruder die that creates lovely little potato gnocchi, or dumplings, complete with perfect ridges and hollows for catching every morsel of sauce. Baking the potatoes results in just the right degree of moisture and lightness so that you shouldn't need to add any additional liquid, but the flour may need to be adjusted slightly as you mix.

Makes about 1 pound

1½ pounds baking potatoes
About 1½ cups all-purpose flour

¾ teaspoon salt

---

1. Preheat the oven to 400 degrees. Pierce the potatoes in one or two places with a fork and bake on a rack in the oven until tender when pierced with the point of a knife, 45 to 60 minutes, depending on size. When cool enough to handle, cut in half, scoop out the potato, and put through a potato ricer. While the potatoes are still slightly warm, place in the mixing container of the pasta machine.

2. Measure the flour by scooping it into a measuring cup and leveling it off with the back of a knife. Sift it into the mixing container of the pasta machine with the salt.

3. Start the machine. Process just until the dough begins to come together, about 1 minute, adding additional flour by tablespoons if necessary. Extrude as directed in the machine's manual.

4. Use the gnocchi immediately or spread out on baking sheets and refrigerate, covered, for up to 8 hours. Or place the gnocchi in a single layer on a baking sheet, freeze until firm, then store in sealed plastic bags in the freezer.

Potato Gnocchi with Fresh Marinara Sauce

4 Servings

3 tablespoons extra-virgin olive oil
5 garlic cloves, crushed through a press
5 cups seeded, chopped tomatoes (about
    4 pounds)
¾ cup dry white wine
3 tablespoons chopped fresh basil
3 tablespoons chopped parsley

1 teaspoon salt
½ teaspoon freshly ground pepper
½ teaspoon sugar
1 recipe Potato Gnocchi
¼ cup imported grated Parmesan cheese,
    plus additional for passing at the table

1. In a large skillet or saucepan, heat the oil over medium heat. Add the garlic and cook, stirring, until fragrant, about 1 minute. Add the tomatoes and wine and cook, stirring occasionally, until the tomatoes give up some of their juices and the sauce begins to thicken, about 10 minutes. Add the basil, parsley, salt, pepper, and sugar. Cook 10 minutes longer.

2. Make the gnocchi and cook about one-third of them at a time in a large pot of boiling salted water until they float, about 2 minutes. Remove each batch with a slotted spoon and keep warm in a shallow serving bowl in a warm oven.

3. Toss the gnocchi with the marinara sauce, sprinkle with the cheese, and toss again. Pass additional cheese at the table.

Potato Gnocchi Gratineed with Sage and Pecorino Romano

Although sage is the traditional choice for this classic sauce, almost any other fresh herb, such as basil, thyme, or marjoram, would be delicious, too. This extremely simple treatment for gnocchi complements and highlights the delicate potato flavor of the dumplings.

4 Servings

---

1 recipe Potato Gnocchi

6 tablespoons butter

2 tablespoons slivered fresh sage leaves or
   2 teaspoons crumbled dried sage

½ cup grated Pecorino Romano cheese

Freshly ground pepper

---

1. Make the gnocchi and cook about one-third of them at a time in a large pot of boiling salted water until they float, about 2 minutes. Remove each batch with a slotted spoon and keep warm in a buttered gratin dish large enough to hold the gnocchi in a more or less even layer.

2. Meanwhile, preheat the broiler. Melt the butter with the sage in a small saucepan over medium heat until the butter foams.

3. Pour the sage butter over the gnocchi and toss to coat. Sprinkle evenly with the cheese. Broil 4 to 5 inches from the heat until the cheese melts and is tinged with brown, 1 to 3 minutes. Watch carefully to avoid scorching.

4. Grind a generous amount of black pepper over the gnocchi and serve.

Saffron Pasta

Saffron, probably the world's most expensive spice, is also one of the strongest, both in flavor and in color. Consequently, it takes only about ½ teaspoon of crushed saffron threads to color a whole batch of pasta a brilliant sunny yellow and imbue it with the distinctive, slightly peppery flavor that is saffron's alone. An equal amount of turmeric will give a similar color, though not much taste.

Makes 1 pound; recommended for all pasta shapes.

---

3 cups all-purpose bleached or unbleached flour

½ teaspoon salt

½ teaspoon crushed saffron threads

2 teaspoons very hot water, plus water as needed

3 "large" eggs

2 teaspoons vegetable oil

---

1. Measure the flour by scooping it into a measuring cup and leveling it off with the back of a knife. Sift it into the mixing container of the pasta machine along with the salt.
2. In a liquid measuring cup, dissolve the saffron in the 2 teaspoons of hot water, allowing it to stand for 5 minutes. Break the eggs into the measuring cup. Add the oil and enough additional water to make ¾ cup. Use a fork or small whisk to lightly beat the eggs. Let stand for 10 minutes to allow the saffron to begin to color the liquid.
3. Start the machine and slowly pour the liquid into the mixing container. Process, adding additional water by tablespoons if needed, and extrude as directed in the machine's manual.
4. Spread the pasta out on wax paper or kitchen towels. Let dry for at least 15 minutes or for up to 2 hours before using. The pasta can be stored in the refrigerator for up to 24 hours or frozen for up to 1 month.

Cioppino with Saffron Linguine

Cioppino is the San Francisco version of bouillabaise. Feel free to change the types of seafood to suit your preference and market availability.

4 Servings

---

1 recipe Saffron Pasta
3 tablespoons extra-virgin olive oil
3 medium leeks (white part only), thinly sliced
1 green bell pepper, chopped
2 garlic cloves, crushed through a press
2 cans "pasta-ready" tomatoes, with their juices
½ cup dry vermouth
½ cup clam juice
2 tablespoons lemon juice

½ teaspoon grated lemon zest
1 teaspoon dried oregano
¾ teaspoon dried thyme
¼ teaspoon freshly ground pepper
¾ pound red snapper fillet, cut into 1-inch chunks
½ pound large shrimp, shelled and deveined
¼ cup chopped flat-leaf parsley
½ pound lump crabmeat, picked over to remove any cartilage or shell

---

1. Cut the pasta into linguine. Let dry on wax paper for at least 15 minutes before using.
2. In a large saucepan, heat the oil. Add the leeks and bell pepper and cook over medium heat, stirring often, until the bell pepper is softened and the leeks are pale golden around the edges, 4 to 6 minutes. Add the garlic and cook, stirring, for 1 minute. Add the tomatoes with their juices, vermouth, clam juice, lemon juice, lemon zest, oregano, thyme, and pepper. Bring to a simmer, reduce the heat to medium-low, partially cover the pot, and simmer for 15 minutes. Add the snapper and shrimp and cook until the shrimp are pink and curled, about 3 minutes. Stir in the parsley and crabmeat. Simmer 1 minute longer.
3. Cook the linguine in a large pot of boiling salted water until tender but still firm, about 2 minutes. Drain in a colander. Divide the linguine among 4 shallow soup dishes. Ladle the seafood and sauce over the linguine and serve at once.

Saffron Cannelloni with Four Cheeses

Gorgeous, golden saffron pasta, with its intense flavor, is used here to enclose a rich filling of ricotta, mozzarella, Parmesan, and tangy Gorgonzola cheeses. The cannelloni are then topped with a chunky sauce and baked, resulting in one of the most elegant meatless main courses we've ever seen.

4 Servings

---

1 recipe Saffron Pasta

All-purpose flour

2 cups ricotta cheese, regular or part-skim

1 cup shredded mozzarella cheese

¼ cup crumbled Gorgonzola or other blue cheese

¼ cup plus 2 tablespoons grated Parmesan cheese

3 tablespoons finely chopped scallions

½ teaspoon grated nutmeg

¼ teaspoon freshly ground pepper

2 cups marinara sauce, homemade or jarred

---

1. Cut the pasta into lasagne noodles about 7 inches long. Sprinkle lightly with flour and use a rolling pin or hand-cranked pasta machine to make sheets about 3 inches wide and 10 inches long. Trim the ragged edges and cut into 3-by-5-inch rectangles. You should have about 16 rectangles. Save any remaining dough for another use. Cook immediately or dust lightly with flour, wrap in plastic, and refrigerate for up to 2 days or freeze for up to 1 month. Thaw in the refrigerator.

2. Cook the pasta rectangles, about 8 at a time, in a large pot of boiling salted water until tender but still firm, about 2 minutes. Drain in a colander and run under cold water to cool. Drain on a towel until ready to use.

3. In a large bowl, whisk together the ricotta, mozzarella, Gorgonzola, ¼ cup of the Parmesan cheese, the scallions, nutmeg, and pepper until well blended.

4. Butter a 9-by-13-inch baking dish. Place the dough rectangles on a flat work surface and spoon 2 tablespoons of the filling lengthwise down the center. Fold both long ends in loosely and place the cannelloni, seam sides down, in a single layer in the prepared dish. Bake immediately or wrap and refrigerate for up to 8 hours. Return to room temperature before baking.

5. Preheat the oven to 400 degrees. Pour the marinara sauce over the cannelloni and sprinkle the remaining 2 tablespoons of Parmesan on top. Bake, uncovered, until the cannelloni are heated through and the sauce is bubbly, 15 to 20 minutes.

Saffron Penne with Fiesta Chorizo and Pepper Sauce

Chorizo is a wonderful, garlicky Spanish sausage that is increasingly available in supermarkets. If you can't find it, use spicy Italian or Portuguese sausage.

4 Servings

---

1 recipe Saffron Pasta
2 tablespoons extra-virgin olive oil
¾ pound chorizo sausage, sliced ¼ inch thick
1 small red bell pepper, thinly sliced
1 small yellow bell pepper, thinly sliced

1 small green bell pepper, thinly sliced
1 large onion, thinly sliced
1 cup chicken broth
1 cup dry white wine
⅓ cup grated Asiago or Parmesan cheese

---

1. Cut the pasta into penne or other short tubular pasta shape. Let dry for at least 15 minutes before using.

2. In a large skillet, heat the oil. Add the sausage and cook over medium-high heat, stirring often, until browned, about 6 minutes. Remove the sausage with a slotted spoon. Add all of the bell peppers and the onion to the drippings in the skillet. Reduce the heat to medium and cook, stirring often, until the vegetables are softened, about 5 minutes. Return the sausage to the pan. Add the broth and wine. Boil, stirring occasionally, until slightly reduced, about 5 minutes.

3. Cook the penne in a large pot of boiling salted water until tender but still firm, 4 to 5 minutes. Drain in a colander. Toss the pasta with the sauce. Sprinkle with the cheese and serve.

Saffron Penne with Tonnato Sauce

Tonnato, or tuna, sauce is one of those great sauces that are concocted from shelf staples that you probably have on hand at all times. (If you don't have canned tuna, anchovies, and stewed tomatoes, run out and stock your pantry right now.)

4 Servings

---

1 recipe Saffron Pasta

2 (6½-ounce) cans tuna packed in olive oil

2 garlic cloves, crushed through a press

2 anchovies

1 (14½-ounce) can Italian-style stewed tomatoes

½ cup clam juice

½ cup dry white wine

½ cup sliced black olives, preferably Niçoise

½ cup chopped flat-leaf parsley

½ teaspoon freshly ground pepper

---

1. Cut the pasta into penne or other similar tubular shape. Let dry on wax paper for at least 15 minutes before using.

2. Meanwhile, drain the oil from the tuna into a large skillet. Add the garlic and cook, stirring, over medium heat until softened, about 1 minute. Add the anchovies and cook, mashing them with the back of a spoon, for 1 minute. Add the stewed tomatoes, clam juice, and wine. Bring to a boil, reduce the heat to medium-low, and simmer until the sauce is slightly thickened, about 8 minutes. Stir in the olives, parsley, pepper, and tuna.

3. Cook the penne in a large pot of boiling lightly salted water until tender but still firm, 3 to 5 minutes. Drain in a colander. Toss the pasta with the sauce, taking care not to break up the tuna too much.

Scallion Pasta

Mild scallions, also known as green onions, give this pasta both a delicate spring green color and a rather sophisticated flavor. Look for slender scallions, which have a more delicate flavor.

Makes 1 pound; recommended for all pasta shapes except angel hair or capellini

---

3 cups all-purpose bleached or unbleached
    flour
½ teaspoon salt
3 "large" eggs

⅓ cup very finely chopped scallions
2 teaspoons vegetable oil
Water

---

1. Measure the flour by scooping it into a measuring cup and leveling it off with the back of a knife. Sift it into the mixing container of the pasta machine along with the salt.
2. Break the eggs into a liquid measuring cup. Add the scallions and oil and enough water to make ¾ cup. Use a fork or small whisk to lightly beat the eggs.
3. Start the machine and slowly pour the liquid into the mixing container. Process, adding additional water by tablespoons if needed, and extrude as directed in the machine's manual.
4. Spread the pasta out on wax paper or kitchen towels. Let dry for at least 15 minutes or for up to 2 hours before using. The pasta can be stored in the refrigerator for up to 24 hours or frozen for up to 1 month.

Scallion Fettuccine with Salmon and Spring Vegetables

Fresh salmon is both delicious and very pretty in this quickly prepared, very delicate mustard sauce over pasta flecked with scallions.

4 Servings

---

1 recipe Scallion Pasta
¾ pound skinless, boneless salmon fillets
12 asparagus spears, preferably pencil-thin
1 cup heavy cream
⅔ cup dry white wine
1 cup frozen baby green peas

¼ cup chopped fresh dill, plus sprigs for garnish
1 tablespoon Dijon mustard
½ teaspoon freshly ground white pepper
Salt

---

1. Cut the pasta into fettuccine. Let dry on wax paper for at least 15 minutes before using. Cut the salmon along the grain into thin strips. Trim the asparagus and cut into 1-inch diagonal pieces.

2. In a medium saucepan, bring the cream and wine just to a boil over medium heat. Add the asparagus, peas, chopped dill, mustard, and white pepper. Reduce the heat to medium-low and simmer 2 minutes. Add the salmon and cook until it is just opaque throughout and the vegetables are crisp-tender, about 2 minutes longer. Season to taste with salt.

3. While the sauce is simmering, cook the fettuccine in a large pot of boiling salted water until tender but still firm, 2 to 3 minutes. Drain in a colander. Toss the pasta with the sauce. Garnish with dill sprigs and serve at once.

Scallion Linguine with Gumbo Sauce

Scallions are a basic ingredient in Cajun and Creole dishes. Here, Scallion Pasta accents a gumbo-style sauce. If you can find real New Orlean's tasso for this recipe, it would be the most authentic ham, but any good smoked ham will work. Filé powder, ground sassafras root, is a common thickener for gumbo. For the best results, it is added near the end of the cooking time.

4 Servings

---

1 recipe Scallion Pasta
4 tablespoons butter
6 ounces tasso or other smoked ham, diced
1½ cups light cream
1 teaspoon dried thyme
¾ teaspoon dried basil

½ teaspoon freshly ground pepper
1 pint (about 18) shucked oysters with their liquor
1 teaspoon filé powder
1 teaspoon Tabasco sauce, or to taste
⅓ cup thinly sliced scallions

---

1. Cut the pasta into linguine. Let dry on wax paper for at least 15 minutes before using.
2. In a large skillet, melt the butter. Add the ham and cook over medium heat, stirring often, until golden, about 4 minutes. Add the cream, thyme, basil, and pepper. Bring to a boil, reduce the heat to medium-low, and simmer until slightly thickened, about 3 minutes. Add the oyster liquor and simmer, stirring occasionally, for 3 minutes longer.
3. Cook the linguine in a large pot of boiling salted water until tender but still firm, about 2 minutes. Drain in a colander.
4. While the pasta is cooking, add the oysters and filé powder to the simmering sauce and cook until the edges of the oysters begin to curl and the sauce thickens slightly, about 2 minutes. Season the sauce with the Tabasco. Gently toss the sauce with the pasta. Sprinkle the scallions on top and serve.

Scallion Penne with Plum Tomato and Smoked Mozzarella Sauce

This summery, no-cook sauce is good with any pasta, but we especially like the mild oniony taste of Scallion Pasta with the freshness of the tomatoes and smoky mozzarella.

4 Servings

1 recipe Scallion Pasta

¼ cup pine nuts

1¼ pounds ripe meaty plum tomatoes, seeded and diced

½ pound smoked mozzarella, cut into ½-inch dice

⅓ cup chopped fresh basil

¼ teaspoon crushed hot pepper flakes

2 garlic cloves, crushed through a press

6 tablespoons extra-virgin olive oil

3 tablespoons balsamic vinegar

1. Cut the pasta into penne. Let dry on wax paper for at least 15 minutes before using.

2. Meanwhile, toast the pine nuts in a dry medium skillet, shaking the pan often, until they are fragrant and lightly browned, about 2 minutes.

3. In a mixing bowl, combine the tomatoes, smoked mozzarella, basil, hot pepper, garlic, oil, and vinegar. Toss to mix. Let stand at least 15 minutes before using.

4. Cook the penne in a large pot of boiling salted water until tender but still firm, 3 to 5 minutes. Drain in a colander. Return the pasta to the hot cooking pot. Add the tomato mixture and the pine nuts. Toss until the cheese is partially melted, about 1 minute. Serve warm or at room temperature.

Scallion Spaghetti with Piquant Picadillo Sauce

4 Servings

---

1 pound ground meat loaf mix or ground
beef or ground pork
1 medium onion, chopped
1 large garlic clove, crushed through a
press
2 teaspoons chili powder
1 teaspoon ground cumin
½ teaspoon dried oregano
¼ teaspoon ground cinnamon
¼ teaspoon ground cloves

¼ teaspoon cayenne
2 (14½-ounce) cans Mexican- or salsa-
style stewed tomatoes
½ cup beef broth
1 (4-ounce) can chopped green chiles
2 tablespoons cider vinegar
¼ cup dried currants or raisins
1 recipe Scallion Pasta
¼ cup chopped or slivered toasted
almonds

---

1. In a large skillet or saucepan, cook the meat and onion over medium heat, stirring often, until the meat loses its red color and the onion is softened, about 7 minutes. Stir in the garlic, chili powder, cumin, oregano, cinnamon, cloves, and cayenne and cook for 1 minute. Add the stewed tomatoes, broth, chiles, vinegar, and currants. Bring to a boil, reduce the heat to medium-low, and simmer, partially covered, for 15 minutes. (The recipe can be made up to 2 days ahead and refrigerated. Reheat before using.)
2. Cut the pasta into thick spaghetti. Let dry on wax paper for at least 15 minutes before using. Cook the thick spaghetti in a large pot of boiling salted water until tender but still firm, about 3 minutes. Drain in a colander
3. Stir the almonds into the picadillo, ladle the sauce over the pasta, and serve.

Spinach Pasta

Fresh cooked spinach can be used, but frozen chopped spinach is so much easier and produces such good results that it is our first choice. Be sure to squeeze out all excess moisture from the spinach. A cheesecloth bag or a fine-mesh strainer works well.

Makes 1 pound; recommended for all pasta shapes

---

3 cups all-purpose bleached or unbleached
    flour
½ teaspoon salt
⅛ teaspoon grated nutmeg
2 "large" eggs

2 teaspoons oil
Water
¼ cup thawed frozen chopped spinach,
    squeezed dry

---

1. Measure the flour by scooping it into a measuring cup and leveling it off with the back of a knife. Sift it into the mixing container of the pasta machine along with the salt and nutmeg.

2. Break the eggs into a liquid measuring cup. Add the oil and enough water to make ½ cup. Pour into a small mixing bowl and add the spinach. Lightly whisk to blend.

3. Start the machine and slowly pour the liquid into the mixing container. Process, adding additional water by tablespoons if needed, and extrude as directed in the machine's manual.

4. Spread the pasta out on wax paper or kitchen towels. Let dry for at least 15 minutes or for up to 2 hours before using. The pasta can be stored in the refrigerator for up to 24 hours or frozen for up to 1 month.

Quick Creamy Spinach and Turkey Lasagne

Traditional Italian lasagnes are often made much as this one, with a creamy sauce rather than a tomato sauce. This delectable and stunning green and white lasagne draws on that classic inspiration, except that we use ground turkey and canned cream soup as tasty shortcuts in the sauce.

8 Servings

---

2 tablespoons olive oil
1 pound ground turkey
1 large onion, chopped
3 garlic cloves, crushed through a press
1 tablespoon dried Italian seasoning
½ cup dry white wine
½ teaspoon salt
½ teaspoon freshly ground black pepper
½ teaspoon freshly ground white pepper

1 (10¾-ounce) can cream of mushroom soup
2 cups part-skim ricotta
1½ cups milk
½ teaspoon grated nutmeg
3 cups grated mozzarella cheese
¼ cup grated Parmesan cheese
1 recipe Spinach Pasta

---

1. In a large skillet, heat the oil. Add the ground turkey, onion, garlic, and Italian seasoning. Cook over medium heat, stirring often, until the turkey browns lightly, about 8 minutes. Add the wine and cook until most of the liquid evaporates, 3 to 4 minutes. Season with the salt, black pepper, and white pepper.

2. In a large bowl, whisk the soup with the ricotta until well blended. Whisk in the milk. Season this white sauce with the nutmeg. Combine the mozzarella and Parmesan in a small bowl.

3. Cut the pasta into lasagne noodles about 6 inches long. Use a rolling pin or hand-cranked pasta machine to roll out to a thickness of about 1/16 inch.

---

4. Spoon 1 cup of the white sauce into a 9-by-13-inch baking dish, tilting to coat the bottom. Layer with one-third of the pasta, trimming to fit if necessary, then half of the turkey mixture and one-third of the white sauce and cheese. Repeat the layering, ending with the last third of the pasta and sauce. Sprinkle with the last of the cheese. Cover with foil. If not baking immediately, refrigerate for up to 24 hours. Return to room temperature before baking.

5. Preheat the oven to 350 degrees. Bake the casserole, covered, for 30 minutes. Uncover and bake until heated through and the cheese is melted, 15 to 20 minutes longer.

Spinach Capellini with Parslied White Clam Sauce

4 Servings

---

1 recipe Spinach Pasta
¼ cup extra-virgin olive oil
2 tablespoons butter
3 large garlic cloves, crushed through a
  press
½ cup chopped scallions
1½ cups clam juice (drained from clams
  plus bottled juice)
⅔ cup dry white wine

1 tablespoon chopped fresh summer savory
  or 1 teaspoon dried
½ teaspoon crushed hot pepper flakes
2 cups drained, chopped fresh clams or 2
  (10-ounce) cans chopped clams,
  drained
1 tablespoon lemon juice
¾ teaspoon grated lemon zest
½ cup chopped flat-leaf parsley

---

1. Cut the pasta into capellini or angel hair. Let dry on wax paper for at least 15 minutes before using.

2. In a large skillet, heat the oil and butter. Add the garlic and scallions and cook over medium heat, stirring constantly, until softened, about 2 minutes. Add the clam juice, wine, summer savory, and hot pepper. Bring just to a boil, reduce the heat to medium-low, and simmer until slightly reduced, about 10 minutes.

3. Add the clams, lemon juice, lemon zest, and parsley. Simmer until the clams are heated through, 1 to 2 minutes.

4. Meanwhile, cook the capellini in a large pot of boiling salted water until tender but still firm, 1 to 2 minutes. Drain in a colander. Toss the pasta with the sauce and serve on rimmed plates to catch the juices.

Paglia e Fieno

A rich sauce for a special occasion, this Italian classic takes its name from the golden "straw" and green "hay" of spinach and egg noodles.

6 Servings

½ recipe Spinach Pasta
½ recipe Basic Egg Pasta
4 tablespoons butter
¾ pound sliced mushrooms, preferably wild mushrooms, such as shiitakes
¼ cup chopped shallots

2 ounces pancetta or smoked ham, finely diced
1 cup frozen baby peas, thawed
2 cups light cream or half-and-half
½ teaspoon freshly ground pepper
¼ cup grated Parmesan cheese

1. Cut both the spinach and egg pasta into fettuccine. Let dry on paper towels for at least 15 minutes before using.

2. In a large skillet, heat the butter. Add the mushrooms, shallots, and pancetta and cook over medium heat, stirring often, until the mushrooms are soft and tinged with brown and the ham is golden, about 5 minutes. Add the peas and cream. Simmer until slightly reduced, about 3 minutes. Season with the pepper and stir in half of the cheese.

3. Cook both pastas in a large pot of boiling salted water until tender but still firm, 2 to 3 minutes. Drain in a colander. Toss the pasta with the sauce. Add the remaining cheese, toss again, and serve.

Mediterranean Eggplant and Garbanzo Bean Spinach Spaghetti

4 Servings

1 small eggplant (about ¾ pound), unpeeled and cut into ¾-inch dice
¾ teaspoon salt
3 tablespoons extra-virgin olive oil
1 large onion, chopped
1 medium green bell pepper, chopped
2 garlic cloves, crushed through a press
2 teaspoons ground cumin
1 teaspoon ground cinnamon
¾ teaspoon ground ginger

¾ teaspoon ground coriander
¼ teaspoon cayenne
1 (28-ounce) can crushed tomatoes in
puree
1 (14½-ounce) can diced tomatoes, with
their juices
1½ cups drained canned garbanzo beans
(chickpeas)
½ cup canned vegetable broth
1 recipe Spinach Pasta

1. Place the eggplant in a colander and sprinkle with the salt. Let stand 15 minutes.
Rinse well under cold water, then pat dry on paper towels.

2. In a large skillet, heat the oil. Add the onion and cook over medium heat, stirring
often, until softened, 3 to 5 minutes. Add the bell pepper and garlic and cook until the
pepper is soft and the onion is beginning to brown, about 5 minutes longer. Stir in the cumin,
cinnamon, ginger, coriander, and cayenne. Cook, stirring, for 1 minute. Add the eggplant,
crushed tomatoes, diced tomatoes with their juices, beans, and broth. Bring to a boil,
cover, reduce the heat to medium-low, and simmer for 20 minutes. Use immediately or
cool and refrigerate for up to 2 days. Reheat before using.

3. Cut the pasta into spaghetti. Let dry on wax paper for at least 15 minutes before
using. Cook the spaghetti in a large pot of boiling salted water until tender but still firm,
2 to 3 minutes. Drain in a colander. Toss the pasta with the sauce.

Spinach Ziti with Two-Tomato and Thyme Sauce

Sun-dried tomatoes give extra potency to bottled marinara sauce. A touch of cream smooths and pulls together both tomato flavors and accents the thyme.

4 Servings

1 recipe Spinach Pasta
½ cup dry red or white wine
2 ounces sun-dried tomatoes, not oil packed
3 tablespoons olive oil
1 large onion, chopped

3 cups bottled or homemade marinara sauce
2 tablespoons chopped fresh thyme or 1½ teaspoons dried
½ cup heavy cream
¼ cup chopped flat-leaf parsley

1. Cut the pasta into ziti or other similar tubular shape. Let dry on wax paper for at least 15 minutes before using.

2. In a small saucepan, bring the wine to a simmer. Remove from the heat and add the sun-dried tomatoes, pushing them into the wine to submerge. Let stand until the tomatoes are softened, about 10 minutes.

3. In a saucepan, heat the oil. Add the onion and cook over medium heat, stirring often, until softened, 3 to 5 minutes. Add the marinara sauce and thyme and simmer 5 minutes. Add the cream and parsley and simmer 5 minutes longer.

4. Cook the ziti in a large pot of boiling salted water until tender but still firm, 3 to 5 minutes. Drain in a colander. Toss the pasta with the sauce and serve.

Sun-Dried Tomato Pasta

With its dusky red color and rich flavor, this pasta can stand on its own sauced only with a little butter or oil and white wine or take to any number of assertive sauces.

Makes 1 pound; recommended for all pasta shapes

---

3 cups all-purpose bleached or unbleached flour

¼ cup (1 ounce) oil-packed sun-dried tomatoes, drained and rinsed

2 "large" eggs

Water

---

1. Measure the flour by scooping it into a measuring cup and leveling it off with the back of a knife. Sift it into the mixing container of the pasta machine.

2. Puree the sun-dried tomatoes in a food processor. Add the eggs and process briefly just to blend. Pour into a liquid measuring cup and add enough water to make ¾ cup.

3. Start the machine and slowly pour the liquid into the mixing container. Process, adding additional water by tablespoons if needed, and extrude as directed in the machine's manual.

4. Spread the pasta out on wax paper or kitchen towels. Let dry for at least 15 minutes or for up to 2 hours before using. The pasta can be stored in the refrigerator for up to 24 hours or frozen for up to 1 month.

Sun-Dried Tomato Rigatoni with White Beans and Broccoli Rabe

Broccoli rabe is a wonderful vegetable in which both the leafy greens and the broccoli-type florets are eminently edible. Greens, beans, and pasta are a terrific (and healthful) combination, and particularly delicious and beautiful with Sun-Dried Tomato Pasta.

4 to 6 Servings

---

1 recipe Sun-Dried Tomato Pasta
¼ cup extra-virgin olive oil
3 large garlic cloves, crushed through a
   press
1 bunch broccoli rabe (about 1 pound),
   coarsely chopped

1½ cups dry white wine
2 (16-ounce) cans white cannellini beans,
   drained and rinsed
½ teaspoon dried summer savory
½ teaspoon coarsely ground black pepper
⅓ cup grated Parmesan cheese

---

1. Cut the pasta into rigatoni or other similar tubular shape. Let dry on wax paper for at least 15 minutes before using.

2. Meanwhile, heat the oil in a large skillet. Add the garlic and cook over medium heat, stirring, for 1 minute. Add the broccoli rabe and cook, stirring, 2 minutes. Add the wine, beans, summer savory, and pepper. Simmer until slightly thickened, about 5 minutes.

3. Cook the rigatoni in a large pot of boiling lightly salted water until tender but still firm, 3 to 5 minutes. Drain in a colander. Toss the pasta with the broccoli rabe sauce. Add the cheese, toss again, and serve.

Wild Mushroom Lasagne with Sun-Dried Tomato Pasta

Three types of mushrooms are combined in this woodsy sauce, which is then layered with savory noodles made with sun-dried tomatoes. The result is a fabulous vegetarian lasagne. Dried mushrooms do add an extra flavor depth, but if you can't get them, increase the amount of shiitakes by 3 or 4 ounces.

8 Servings

---

1 cup dry white wine

2 ounces dried mushrooms (any type)

2 tablespoons olive oil

1 medium onion, chopped

3 garlic cloves, crushed through a press

8 ounces white button mushrooms, sliced

4 ounces shiitake mushrooms, stemmed, caps sliced

4 cups spicy red pepper tomato sauce (see Note)

1 recipe Sun-Dried Tomato Pasta

2 cups shredded mozzarella cheese

1 cup shredded Cheddar cheese

½ cup grated Parmesan cheese

2 cups ricotta, regular or part-skim

---

1. In a small nonreactive saucepan, bring the wine just to a boil. Add the mushrooms, remove from the heat, and let steep for 30 minutes. Drain well, reserving the soaking liquid. Chop the mushrooms. Strain the soaking liquid through a coffee filter or fine-mesh sieve and set aside.

2. Heat the oil in a large skillet over medium heat. Add the onion and cook, stirring frequently, until softened, 3 to 5 minutes. Add the garlic and sliced mushrooms. Continue to cook, stirring frequently, until the mushrooms are soft and have given up their liquid, about 5 minutes. Add the tomato sauce, chopped dried mushrooms, and reserved soaking liquid. Simmer, uncovered, until slightly reduced and thickened, about 10 minutes.

3. Cut the pasta into lasagne noodles about 6 inches long. Use a rolling pin or hand-cranked pasta machine to roll out to a thickness of about 1/16 inch. In a bowl, toss together the mozzarella, Cheddar, and Parmesan cheeses.

4. Spoon 1 cup of the sauce into a 3- to 4-quart shallow baking dish, tilting to coat the buttom. Layer with one-third of the pasta, trimming it to fit if necessary, then one-half of the ricotta and one-third of the mixed cheeses. Spoon one-third of the sauce over the cheese. Repeat the layering, ending with the last third of the pasta and sauce. Sprinkle with the remaining cheese. Cover with foil. If not baking immediately, refrigerate for up to 24 hours. Return to room temperature before baking.

5. Preheat the oven to 350 degrees. Bake the casserole, covered, for 30 minutes. Uncover and bake until heated through and the cheese is melted, 15 to 20 minutes longer.

NOTE: There are a couple of good bottled tomato sauces flavored with red pepper. If you cannot find one, add ¼ teaspoon cayenne to a good-quality chunky bottled marinara sauce.

Sun-Dried Tomato Spaghetti Carbonara

Pancetta, a key ingredient in spaghetti carbonara, is an unsmoked Italian bacon found in specialty food stores. If you can't find it, use regular bacon, but boil it first in a pot of boiling water for about 1 minute to remove some of the smokiness.

4 Servings

---

1 recipe Sun-Dried Tomato Pasta
6 ounces pancetta, thinly sliced and cut into strips
2 tablespoons extra-virgin olive oil
2 whole eggs

2 egg whites
½ cup chicken broth
½ cup grated Parmesan cheese
⅓ cup chopped parsley
1 teaspoon coarsely ground black pepper

---

1. Cut the pasta into thick spaghetti, preferably perciatelli. Let dry on wax paper for at least 15 minutes before using.

2. Meanwhile, in a large skillet, cook the pancetta in the oil over medium heat until golden, about 3 minutes. In a mixing bowl, whisk together the whole eggs, egg whites, and broth.

3. Cook the spaghetti in a large pot of boiling lightly salted water until tender but still firm, 3 to 4 minutes. Drain and then immediately add to the hot skillet along with the egg mixture. Toss to coat the spaghetti with the egg mixture. Cook, tossing over low heat, for 2 minutes. Add half of the cheese, half of the parsley, and all of the pepper. Toss again. Serve at once, with the remaining cheese and parsley sprinkled on top.

Sun-Dried Tomato Spaghettini with Arugula and Bacon

Arugula has a peppery flavor that is wonderful with the saltiness of bacon and the rich flavor of Sun-Dried Tomato Pasta. The canned tomatoes pull all the flavors together to make a sophisticated little supper dish that goes together in minutes.

4 Servings

---

1 recipe Sun-Dried Tomato Pasta
6 slices of bacon
2 tablespoons extra-virgin olive oil
2 garlic cloves, crushed through a press
6 cups slivered arugula (2 or 3 bunches)
1 (14½-ounce) can diced tomatoes, with their juices

½ cup dry white wine
⅓ cup chicken broth
⅓ cup grated Romano cheese
½ teaspoon freshly ground pepper

---

1. Cut the pasta into spaghettini or other thin spaghetti. Let dry on wax paper for at least 15 minutes before using.

2. Meanwhile, in a large skillet, cook the bacon over medium heat until crisp, about 5 minutes. Drain on paper towels, then coarsely crumble and reserve. Pour off all but 2 tablespoons of the bacon drippings and add the oil to the skillet. Add the garlic and arugula and cook over medium heat, stirring, until the arugula is wilted, about 2 minutes. Add the tomatoes with their juices, wine, and broth. Bring to a boil and cook, stirring often, until slightly reduced, about 5 minutes.

3. Cook the spaghettini in a large pot of boiling lightly salted water until tender but still firm, about 2 minutes. Drain in a colander. Toss the pasta with the sauce. Add the cheese and pepper, toss again, and serve.

Tomato Pasta

The difference between this and Sun-Dried Tomato Pasta is the more delicate flavor and brighter color imparted by the tomato paste.

Makes 1 pound; recommended for all pasta shapes

---

3 cups all-purpose bleached or unbleached flour
½ teaspoon salt
2 "large" eggs

¼ cup tomato paste
2 teaspoons olive oil
Water

---

1. Measure the flour by scooping it into a measuring cup and leveling it off with the back of a knife. Sift it into the mixing container of the pasta machine along with the salt.
2. Break the eggs into a liquid measuring cup. Add the tomato paste, oil, and enough water to make ¾ cup plus 1 tablespoon. Use a fork or small whisk to lightly beat the eggs.
3. Start the machine and slowly pour the liquid into the mixing container. Process, adding additional water by tablespoons if needed, and extrude as directed in the machine's manual.
4. Spread the pasta out on wax paper or kitchen towels. Let dry for at least 15 minutes or for up to 2 hours before using. The pasta can be stored in the refrigerator for up to 24 hours or frozen for up to 1 month.

Tomato Fettuccine with Mixed Mushroom Sauce

4 Servings

1 recipe Tomato Pasta
1 cup chicken broth
2 ounces dried wild mushrooms, preferably
   morels
2 tablespoons butter
¾ pound fresh wild mushrooms, such as
   a mix of shiitake and cremini, thickly
   sliced
1 large garlic clove, crushed through a
   press

⅓ cup chopped shallots
1 tablespoon chopped fresh tarragon or
   1 teaspoon dried
1 cup heavy cream
½ cup dry white wine
¼ cup Madeira or dry sherry
Salt and freshly ground pepper

1. Cut the pasta into fettuccine. Let dry on wax paper for at least 15 minutes before using. Meanwhile, bring the broth to a boil and pour it over the dried mushrooms in a small heatproof bowl. Let stand at least 15 minutes, until the mushrooms are softened. Remove the mushrooms and coarsely chop. Strain the liquid through a coffe filter or cheesecloth; reserve separately.

2. In a large frying pan, heat the butter and cook the fresh mushrooms, garlic, and shallots over medium heat, stirring often, until the mushrooms are softened, about 5 minutes. Add the tarragon, cream, and wine. Bring to a boil, reduce the heat to medium-low, and simmer, stirring often, until the mushrooms are very soft, about 10 minutes. Add the Madeira, dried mushrooms, and soaking liquid. Simmer for 3 minutes. Season with salt and pepper to taste.

3. Cook the fettuccine in a large pot of boiling salted water until tender but still firm, 2 to 3 minutes. Drain in a colander. Toss the pasta with the sauce and serve.

Tomato Macaroni with Cheddar and Ale Sauce

4 Servings

1 recipe Tomato Pasta
3 tablespoons butter
3 tablespoons all-purpose flour
1 teaspoon dry mustard
1¾ cups milk
¾ cup ale or beer
3 cups shredded medium-sharp Cheddar
   cheese (about ¾ pound)

1 teaspoon Worcestershire sauce
¼ teaspoon cayenne
¼ cup chopped pimiento
¼ cup thinly sliced scallion greens
½ teaspoon paprika

1. Cut the pasta into macaroni. Let dry on wax paper for at least 15 minutes before using.
2. In a medium saucepan, melt the butter over medium-low heat. Stir in the flour and mustard until smooth. Cook, stirring, for 2 minutes. Gradually whisk in the milk. Raise the heat to medium-high and bring to a boil, stirring constantly. Reduce the heat to medium, add the ale, and cook for 3 minutes. Remove the pan from the heat and add the cheese in 3 handfuls, stirring until each handful is melted before adding another. Stir in the Worcestershire, cayenne, and pimiento.
3. Cook the macaroni in a large pot of boiling salted water until tender but still firm, 3 to 4 minutes. Drain in a colander. Toss the pasta with the sauce. Sprinkle the scallions and paprika over each serving.

Tomato Rigatoni with Herbed Eggplant and Sicilian Olive Sauce

4 Servings

1 recipe Tomato Pasta
2 small eggplants (about ¾ pound each), peeled and cut into ¾-inch cubes
Salt
¼ cup extra-virgin olive oil
1 medium onion, chopped
1 (14½-ounce) can diced tomatoes, with their juices
3 garlic cloves, crushed through a press

1 teaspoon dried thyme
½ cup dry white wine
½ cup chicken broth
½ cup heavy cream
½ cup sliced olives, preferably Sicilian
⅓ cup thinly sliced fresh basil
Freshly ground pepper
¼ cup grated Parmesan cheese

1. Cut the pasta into rigatoni or other similar shape. Let dry on wax paper for at least 15 minutes before using. Meanwhile, place the eggplant in a large colander, sprinkle generously with salt, and let stand for at least 15 minutes. Rinse the eggplant thoroughly under cold water, then pat it dry on paper towels.

2. In a large skillet, heat the oil. Add the eggplant and onion and cook over medium heat, stirring often, until the eggplant begins to brown and the onion is softened, about 5 minutes. Add the tomatoes with their juices, garlic, and thyme. Cook, stirring, for 3 minutes. Add the wine and broth and simmer for 3 minutes longer. Add the cream, olives, and basil. Reduce the heat to medium-low and simmer until the eggplant is very soft, about 5 minutes. Season with pepper.

3. Cook the rigatoni in a large pot of boiling salted water until tender but still firm, 3 to 5 minutes; drain. Toss the pasta with the sauce. Sprinkle with the cheese and serve.

Tomato Ziti with Mediterranean Lamb, Chickpeas, and Zucchini

4 Servings

1 recipe Tomato Pasta
2 tablespoons olive oil
¾ pound lean boneless lamb, cut into
  1-inch cubes
1 large onion, chopped
2 large garlic cloves, crushed through a
  press
1 teaspoon ground cumin
¼ teaspoon ground cinnamon

¼ teaspoon cayenne
2 (14½-ounce) cans stewed tomatoes
½ cup dry red wine
2 medium zucchini (about ¾ pound
  total), diced
1 cup drained canned chickpeas (garbanzo
  beans)
¼ cup chopped fresh mint
Salt and freshly ground pepper

1. Cut the pasta into ziti or other similar tubular shape. Let dry on wax paper for at least 15 minutes before using.

2. In a large skillet, heat the oil. Add the lamb and onion and cook over medium-high heat, stirring occasionally, until the lamb is browned, 5 to 7 minutes. Add the garlic and cook for 30 seconds. Stir in the cumin, cinnamon, and cayenne. Add the tomatoes and wine. Bring to a boil, reduce the heat to medium-low, and cook, uncovered, until the meat is tender and the sauce is slightly reduced, about 20 minutes. Add the zucchini, garbanzos, and mint. Cook until the zucchini is just tender, about 3 minutes. Stir in the mint. Season to taste with salt and pepper.

3. Cook the ziti in a large pot of boiling salted water until tender but still firm, 3 to 5 minutes. Drain in a colander. Toss the pasta with the sauce and serve.

Wild Mushroom Pasta

While this recipe was developed with porcini mushrooms, any kind of dried wild mushrooms can be used. The depth of the brown color will depend upon the color of the mushrooms. This is an assertively flavored pasta, so use it with equally potent and earthy sauces, or try no sauce at all save a light coating of olive oil and chopped garlic.

Makes 1 pound; recommended for all pasta shapes except angel hair or capellini

---

1 ounced dried mushrooms, such as porcini
¼ cup boiling water
3 cups all-purpose bleached or unbleached flour

½ teaspoon salt
2 "large" eggs
2 teaspoons olive oil
Water

---

1. Put the mushrooms in a measuring cup and pour the boiling water over them, pressing the mushrooms to submerge them in the water. Let stand until the mushrooms are softened, about 20 minutes. Spoon the mushrooms into a food processor. Strain the soaking liquid into the processor, taking care not to pour in any sediment left in the bottom of the measuring cup. Puree the mushrooms.

2. Measure the flour by scooping it into a measuring cup and leveling off it with the back of a knife. Sift it into the mixing container of the pasta machine along with the salt.

3. Break the eggs into a liquid measuring cup. Add the mushroom puree, oil, and enough water to make ¾ cup. Use a fork or small whisk to lightly beat the eggs.

4. Start the machine and slowly pour the liquid into the mixing container. Process, adding additional water by tablespoons if needed, and extrude as directed in the machine's manual.

5. Spread the pasta out on wax paper or kitchen towels. Let dry for at least 15 minutes or for up to 2 hours before using. The pasta can be stored in the refrigerator for up to 24 hours or frozen for up to 1 month.

Wild Mushroom Capellini with Prosciutto and Roasted Pepper Puree

For this recipe, it is worth roasting the peppers yourself, for the smoky sweetness is the true essence of this brilliant red-orange sauce.

4 Servings

---

1 recipe Wild Mushroom Pasta
1 pound red bell peppers (about 3)
1 large shallot, peeled
2 tablespoons tomato paste
1 tablespoon balsamic vinegar
¼ teaspoon sugar

½ cup extra-virgin olive oil
½ teaspoon Tabasco sauce
Salt
2 ounces thinly sliced prosciutto, slivered
3 tablespoons slivered fresh basil

---

1. Cut the pasta into capellini. Let dry on wax paper for at least 15 minutes before using.
2. Roast the peppers by setting them under a broiler, over a gas flame, or on a grill and turning occasionally until they are blackened all over, about 10 minutes. Place the peppers in a paper bag or wrap in aluminum foil. Let them stand for about 10 minutes to steam off the skins. Unwrap and peel off the skins, then remove the ribs and seeds.
3. Place the peppers in a food processor along with the shallot, tomato paste, vinegar, and sugar. Process to make a coarse puree, about 10 seconds. With the machine on, slowly pour in 6 tablespoons of the oil to make a smooth puree. Season with the Tabasco and salt to taste. (The pepper sauce can be made up to 2 days ahead and refrigerated.) When ready to serve, gently warm the puree in a saucepan set over medium-low heat.
4. In a large skillet, cook the prosciutto in the remaining 2 tablespoons oil over medium-high heat, stirring often, until just golden, about 3 minutes. Remove the skillet from the heat.

---

5. Cook the capellini in a large pot of boiling salted water until tender but still firm, about 1 minute. Drain in a colander. Add the pasta along with the basil to the skillet with the prosciutto. Toss to coat with the oil.

6. To serve, swirl the pasta into large "nests," 2 on each serving plate. Ladle the warm pepper puree into the center of the nests.

Wild Mushroom Rigatoni with Red Beans and Winter Savory Sauce

4 to 6 Servings

1 recipe Wild Mushroom Pasta
4 slices of thick-cut bacon
1 large onion, coarsely chopped
1 green bell pepper, coarsely chopped
1 large garlic clove, crushed through a
   press
2 (14½-ounce) cans stewed tomatoes

1 (14- to 16-ounce) can red kidney
   beans, drained and rinsed
1½ teaspoons dried savory
¾ teaspoon dried oregano
½ teaspoon dried thyme
½ teaspoon salt
½ teaspoon freshly ground black pepper

1. Cut the pasta into rigatoni or other similar tubular shape. Let dry on wax paper for at least 15 minutes before using.

2. In a large skillet, cook the bacon over medium heat until crisp, about 5 minutes. Drain on paper towels. Crumble the bacon and reserve it. Add the onion, bell pepper, and garlic to the drippings in the skillet. Cook over medium heat, stirring often, until the vegetables are softened, about 5 minutes. Add the stewed tomatoes, beans, savory, oregano, thyme, salt, and pepper. Bring to a boil, reduce the heat to medium-low, partially cover, and simmer until slightly thickened, about 10 minutes.

3. Cook the rigatoni in a large pot of boiling salted water until tender but still firm, 3 to 5 minutes. Drain in a colander. Ladle the sauce over the pasta and serve.

Chicken Cacciatore
over Wild Mushroom Spaghetti

4 Servings

1 recipe Wild Mushroom Pasta

1 pound skinless, boneless chicken thighs, cut into thick, ½-inch-wide strips

Salt and freshly ground pepper

3 tablespoons olive oil

2 Italian green frying peppers, thinly sliced

1 large onion, thinly sliced

2 garlic cloves, crushed through a press

1 (14½-ounce) can Italian-style stewed tomatoes

½ cup dry red wine

½ cup chicken broth

1 bay leaf, broken in half

1 teaspoon dried rosemary

½ teaspoon dried marjoram

½ teaspoon grated lemon zest

¼ cup chopped flat-leaf parsley

1. Cut the pasta into spaghetti. Let dry on wax paper for at least 15 minutes before using.
2. Season the chicken lightly with salt and pepper. In a large skillet, heat 2 tablespoons of the oil. Add the chicken and cook over medium-high heat, turning often, until golden all over, 6 to 8 minutes. Remove with tongs. Reduce the heat to medium, add the remaining oil to the skillet, and cook the peppers and onion, stirring often, until the vegetables are softened, about 5 minutes. Add the garlic and cook for 30 seconds. Stir in the tomatoes, wine, broth, bay leaf, rosemary, marjoram, and lemon zest. Bring just to a boil, reduce the heat to medium-low, return the chicken to the pan, and simmer until the sauce is slightly thickened and the chicken is tender, about 10 minutes. Discard the bay leaf.
3. Cook the spaghetti in a large pot of boiling salted water until tender but still firm, 2 to 3 minutes. Drain in a colander. Spoon the sauce over the spaghetti. Sprinkle with the parsley.

Chinese Egg Noodles

These rich, golden noodles are great with a wide variety of sauces. This is also the preferred dough for won ton wrappers and other Asian dumplings.

Makes 1 pound; use for angel hair, regular spaghetti, linguine, and fettuccine-width Asian noodles as well as for won ton wrappers

---

3 cups all-purpose bleached or unbleached
    flour
½ teaspoon salt
⅓ cup milk

3 "large" egg yolks
Water
Cornstarch

---

1. Measure the flour by scooping it into a measuring cup and leveling it off with the back of a knife. Sift it into the mixing container of the pasta machine along with the salt.
2. Measure the milk in a glass measuring cup. Add the egg yolks and lightly beat with a fork or small whisk. Add enough water to make ¾ cup.
3. Start the machine and slowly pour the liquid into the mixing container. Process, adding additional water by tablespoons if necessary, and extrude as directed in the machine's manual.
4. Spread the noodles on wax paper or kitchen towels and let dry for at least 15 minutes or for up to 2 hours before using. Sprinkle lightly with cornstarch to prevent stickiness. Store in the refrigerator for up to 24 hours or freeze for up to 1 month.

Stir-Fried Pork and Black Bean Sauce with Chinese Egg Noodles

Intensely dark and flavorful, Chinese black bean sauce is made from preserved black beans and ginger, sesame, sherry, and garlic. It can be found in jars in Asian markets and in many supermarkets. If you can't find it, substitute hoisin sauce. The flavor will not be the same, but it will taste equally good.

4 Servings

---

1 recipe Chinese Egg Noodles
1 tablespoon peanut or other vegetable oil
1 pound lean boneless pork, cut into thin strips
¾ teaspoon freshly ground pepper
¼ cup bottled Chinese black bean sauce
1½ tablespoons soy sauce

1 tablespoon Asian sesame oil
1 tablespoon rice wine vinegar
1 tablespoon sugar
¾ cup chopped roasted peanuts
1 bunch of scallions, thinly sliced
½ cup chopped cilantro

---

1. Cut the noodle dough into thin spaghetti. Let dry on wax paper for at least 15 minutes before using. Cook in a large pot of boiling salted water until tender but still firm, about 2 minutes. Drain in a colander, rinse with water to remove the starch, and set aside.

2. Heat the oil in a large skillet or wok. Season the pork with the pepper and stir-fry over high heat until the meat is no longer pink, 2 to 3 minutes. Reduce the heat to medium and add the black bean sauce, soy sauce, sesame oil, vinegar, sugar, and 1 cup of water. Cook, stirring, until the sugar dissolves, about 1 minute.

3. Add the noddles to the sauce and toss until coated and heated through, about 2 minutes. Pass the peanuts, scallions, and cilantro in small bowls at the table for sprinkling on top.

Chinese Cold Sesame Noodles

Soft noodles, smoky-garlicky sesame dressing, crunchy scallions, and lettuce all add up to this all-time favorite salad. Serve it on its own or as a side dish to cooked meat or chicken.

4 to 6 Servings

---

1 recipe Chinese Egg Noodles
¼ cup red wine vinegar
3 tablespoons soy sauce
2 garlic cloves, smashed
1 tablespoon chopped fresh ginger
1 tablespoon sugar
½ teaspoon crushed hot pepper flakes

¼ teaspoon freshly ground black pepper
¼ cup peanut oil
3 tablespoons Asian sesame oil
1 bunch of scallions, thinly sliced
5 cups coarsely shredded romaine lettuce
¼ cup toasted sesame seeds

---

1. Cut the noodle dough into thin spaghetti or thin linguine. Let dry on wax paper for at least 15 minutes before using. Cook in a large pot of boiling salted water until tender but still firm, about 2 minutes. Drain in a colander and rinse under cold water to remove excess starch; drain well.

2. In a blender or food processor, combine the vinegar, soy sauce, garlic, ginger, sugar, hot pepper, and black pepper. With the machine on, pour the peanut oil and sesame oil through the feed tube and process until smooth.

3. In a large bowl, toss the sauce with the noodles and scallions. Refrigerate for at least 30 minutes or for up to 4 hours.

4. To serve, make a bed of lettuce on a serving platter. Mound the noodles on the lettuce. Garnish with the sesame seeds. Serve chilled.

Cold Peanut Noodle Salad

With its creamy, hot peanut dressing, this salad is great just on its own as a meatless main course or as a side dish to grilled lamb or chicken and vegetables.

4 to 6 Servings

---

1 recipe Chinese Egg Noodles
4 ounces snow peas, strings removed
½ cup peanut butter, creamy or chunky
¼ cup soy sauce
3 tablespoons red wine vinegar
2 tablespoons lime juice
1 tablespoon sugar
1½ tablespoons chopped fresh ginger

2 garlic cloves, peeled
¾ teaspoon crushed hot pepper flakes
3 tablespoons peanut oil
2 tablespoons Asian sesame oil
½ cup vegetable broth or water
Romaine lettuce leaves
1 bunch of scallions, thinly sliced

---

1. Cut the noodle dough into linguine. Let dry on wax paper for at least 15 minutes before using. Cook in a large pot of boiling salted water until tender but still firm, 2 to 3 minutes. Add the snow peas during the last 30 seconds of cooking time. Drain the noodles and snow peas in a colander and rinse under cold water to remove the starch; drain well.

2. In a food processor, combine the peanut butter, soy sauce, vinegar, lime juice, sugar, ginger, garlic, and hot pepper. With the machine on, pour the peanut oil, sesame oil, and broth through the feed tube. Process until smooth.

3. Pour the sauce over the noodles and snow peas and toss to coat well. Cover and refrigerate for at least 30 minutes or for up to 4 hours.

4. To serve, arrange the lettuce leaves on a serving platter. Mound the noodle salad over the lettuce. Garnish with the scallions. Serve chilled.

Vietnamese Chicken Noodle Salad
with Lime-Mint Dressing

When fresh mint is in high season, make this colorful and cooling noodle salad. In both Vietnam and Thailand, a bottled fish-based sauce called nam pla *lays the groundwork for seasoning many, many dishes. Fortunately for us, this delicious condiment is increasingly available in this country.*

4 Servings

Lime-Mint Dressing (recipe follows)
1 pound skinless, boneless chicken breasts
½ recipe Chinese Egg Noodles
1 red bell pepper, chopped

1 yellow bell pepper, chopped
½ cup chopped roasted peanuts
1 bunch of scallions, thinly sliced
Mint sprigs, for garnish

---

1. In a shallow dish, pour ¼ cup of the Lime-Mint Dressing over the chicken; turn to coat both sides. Set aside to marinate for at least 15 minutes at room temperature or for up to 4 hours in the refrigerator.

2. Cut the noodle dough into thin linguine. Let dry on wax paper for at least 15 minutes before using. Cook in a large pot of boiling salted water until tender but still firm, about 2 minutes. Drain in a colander and rinse under cold running water to remove the starch; drain well.

3. Prepare a medium-hot fire in a charcoal or gas grill. Grill the chicken, turning once or twice, until the meat is white throughout but still juicy, 8 to 10 minutes.

4. Toss the cooked noodles and the chopped peppers with the remaining Lime-Mint Dressing. Cut the grilled chicken crosswise into slices and arrange over the salad. Sprinkle the chopped peanuts and scallions on top and garnish with mint sprigs.

Lime-Mint Dressing

Makes about 1 cup

¼ cup Vietnamese or Thai fish sauce
  (*nam pla*)
1 teaspoon grated lime zest
¼ cup fresh lime juice
1 tablespoon soy sauce
1 teaspoon sugar

2 garlic cloves, crushed through a press
½ teaspoon crushed hot pepper flakes
6 tablespoons peanut or other vegetable
  oil
⅓ cup chopped fresh mint

In a small bowl, whisk together the fish sauce, lime zest, lime juice, soy sauce, sugar, garlic, and hot pepper. Whisk in the oil and stir in the mint.

Chicken Noodle Salad
with Lemongrass Vinaigrette

Lemongrass has a heavenly, tangy, citrus flavor that is unique. The plant has a fibrous, woody stem, which must be very finely minced when used in a dressing. If you can't find lemongrass, substitute 2 teaspoons grated lemon zest in this dressing.

4 Servings

---

2 tablespoons white wine vinegar
1 tablespoon soy sauce
1 tablespoon finely minced lemongrass
6 tablespoons olive oil
½ teaspoon Tabasco sauce
½ recipe Chinese Egg Noodles
3 cups diced cooked chicken (about 12 ounces)

1 medium red bell pepper, cut into thin strips
1½ cups bean sprouts
½ cup slivered red onion
¼ cup chopped cilantro
3 to 4 large leaves of Napa cabbage or romaine lettuce

---

1. In a small bowl, whisk together the vinegar, soy sauce, lemongrass, olive oil, and Tabasco. Cover and refrigerate until ready to use.

2. Cut the noodle dough into linguine. Let dry on wax paper for at least 15 minutes before using. Cook in a large pot of boiling salted water until tender but still firm, 2 to 3 minutes. Drain in a colander and rinse well with cold water to remove the starch; drain well.

3. In a large bowl, combine the noodles with the chicken, bell pepper, bean sprouts, red onion, and half the cilantro. Add the dressing and toss to coat well. Serve immediately or refrigerate for up to 2 hours.

4. Arrange a bed of the cabbage leaves on a platter and spread the salad over the leaves. Sprinkle with the remaining cilantro before serving.

Won Ton Soup

½ pound lean boneless pork, cut into
   1-inch cubes
3 water chestnuts
1 tablespoon soy sauce
1 tablespoon dry sherry
1 tablespoon coarsely chopped fresh ginger
1 garlic clove, smashed

¼ teaspoon cayenne
½ recipe Chinese Egg Noodles
Cornstarch
8 cups chicken broth, homemade or
   reduced-sodium
3 scallions, thinly sliced

1. In a food processor, combine the pork, water chestnuts, soy sauce, sherry, ginger, garlic, and cayenne. Use long pulses to grind to a smooth paste. Use the filling immediately or refrigerate for up to 24 hours.

2. Cut the dough into lasagne noodles about 7 inches long. Sprinkle lightly with cornstarch and use a rolling pin or hand-cranked pasta machine to roll the pasta into thin sheets 3 inches wide. Cut into 32 (3-inch) squares. If not using immediately, dust with cornstarch, cover with plastic wrap, and refrigerate for up to 24 hours.

3. To make the won tons, arrange the wrappers on a work surface. Place 1 teaspoon of filling in the center of each square. Brush the edges of each square with water to moisten. Fold diagonally into a triangle and press the edges to seal well. Bring the 2 bottom points of the triangle together and pinch to join. Cook the won tons immediately or cover lightly and refrigerate for up to 12 hours. To freeze, arrange on a baking sheet, freeze until firm, then transfer to a plastic bag and store in the freezer.

4. In a large soup pot, bring the chicken broth to a boil. Add the won tons and simmer, partially covered, over medium to medium-low heat until the dough is tender and the filling loses its pink color, 5 to 8 minutes. Ladle the soup into bowls and garnish with the scallions.

Curried Chicken Pot Stickers

These famous northern Chinese dumplings, called "pot stickers," are pan-fried until the bottoms are crisp and then steamed until tender. A sauce is added for the last few minutes of cooking, so that the dumplings are finished with a lovely shiny glaze. Pot stickers are traditionally served as an appetizer, but along with some vegetables and a salad, they can make a terrific light meal.

Makes 32 pot stickers; 4 to 6 servings

½ pound skinless, boneless chicken breast, cut into 1-inch chunks

3 water chestnuts

2 scallions, cut into 1-inch lengths

1 tablespoon coarsely chopped fresh ginger

1 tablespoon soy sauce

1¾ teaspoons curry powder

¼ teaspoon cayenne

½ recipe Chinese Egg Noodles

Cornstarch

½ cup chicken broth

¼ cup unsweetened canned coconut milk

2 tablespoons dry sherry

½ teaspoon sugar

2 tablespoons peanut or vegetable oil

---

1. In a food processor, combine the chicken, water chestnuts, scallions, ginger, soy sauce, 1½ teaspoons of the curry powder, and the cayenne. Use long pulses to grind to a smooth paste. Use the filling immediately or refrigerate for up to 24 hours.

2. Cut the dough into lasagne noodles about 7 inches long. Sprinkle lightly with cornstarch and use a rolling pin or hand-cranked pasta machine to roll the pasta into thin sheets 3 inches wide. Use a 3-inch cookie or biscuit cutter to cut the dough into 32 rounds. If not using immediately, dust with cornstarch, cover with plastic wrap, and refrigerate for up to 24 hours.

3. To make the pot stickers, arrange the wrappers on a flat work surface. Place 1 teaspoon of filling in the center of each round of dough. Brush the edges of the wrappers with water to moisten. Fold over into a half-moon shape and press the edges to seal. Make several small pleats in the seal. Cook immediately or cover lightly and refrigerate for up to 8 hours. To freeze, arrange on a baking sheet, freeze until firm, then transfer to a plastic bag and store in the freezer.

4. In a small bowl, whisk together the chicken broth, coconut milk, sherry, sugar, and remaining ¼ teaspoon curry powder. Set the sauce aside.

5. In a large skillet, preferably nonstick, heat the oil over medium-high heat. Add the dumplings and cook, uncovered, until their bottoms are golden brown, 2 to 3 minutes. Add the sauce to the pan. Cover, reduce the heat to medium-low, and steam until the dough is tender, 4 to 5 minutes.

6. Uncover the pan, raise the heat to medium-high, and boil until the sauce is reduced by about half and there is no trace of pink in the chicken filling, 2 to 3 minutes. Spoon the reduced sauce over the pot stickers until they are glazed. Transfer to a platter and serve while they're hot.

Szechuan Shrimp Dumplings with Fireball Dipping Sauce

Makes 32 dumplings; 4 to 6 servings

½ pound shelled and deveined shrimp
4 water chestnuts
1 garlic clove, smashed
1 tablespoon dry sherry
1 teaspoon cornstarch
½ teaspoon Asian sesame oil
½ teaspoon salt

½ teaspoon ground Szechuan peppercorns
  or white pepper
½ recipe Chinese Egg Noodles
Cornstarch
¼ cup soy sauce
2 teaspoons Chinese chili oil
3 scallions, thinly sliced

---

1. In a food processor, combine the shrimp, water chestnuts, garlic, sherry, cornstarch, sesame oil, salt, and Szechuan peppercorns. Use long pulses to grind to a smooth paste. Use the filling immediately or refrigerate for up to 24 hours.

2. Cut the dough into lasagne noodles about 7 inches long. Sprinkle lightly with cornstarch and use a rolling pin or hand-cranked pasta machine to roll the pasta into thin sheets 3 inches wide. Cut into 32 (3-inch) squares. If not using immediately, dust with cornstarch, cover with plastic wrap, and refrigerate for up to 24 hours.

3. To make the dumplings, arrange the wrappers on a flat work surface. Place 1 teaspoon of filling in the center of each square. Brush the edges of each square with water to moisten. Fold diagonally into a triangle and press the edges to seal. Bring the 2 bottom points of the triangle together and pinch to join. Cook the dumplings immediately or cover lightly and refrigerate for up to 12 hours. To freeze, arrange the dumplings on a large baking sheet, freeze them until firm, then transfer them to a plastic bag. Seal tightly and store in the freezer.

4. Assemble a bamboo or regular metal steamer, fill with water, and bring to a boil. (If

---

using a metal steamer, oil the basket.) Arrange the dumplings in the steamer basket and cook, covered, over medium heat until the dumplings are tender and the filling is cooked through, about 10 minutes.

5. In a small bowl, combine the soy sauce, chili oil, and scallions. Serve the hot dumplings, with the sauce for dipping.

Japanese Udon Noodles

*These traditional Japanese noodles are made with high-gluten bread flour. The dough
is mixed a bit longer than most to produce a pleasantly chewy noodle.*

Makes 1 pound; recommended for spaghetti and linguine

---

3 cups bread flour   About ¾ cup water
1 teaspoon salt

---

1. Measure the flour by scooping it into a measuring cup and leveling it off with the
back of a knife. Sift it into the mixing container of the pasta machine along with the salt.
2. Start the machine and slowly pour ¾ cup water into the mixing container. Process,
adding additional water by tablespoons if necessary, and extrude as directed in the machine's manual.
3. Spread the noodles out on wax paper or kitchen towels and sprinkle lightly with flour
to prevent sticking. Let dry for at least 15 minutes or for up to 8 hours before cooking.
The noodles can be stored, covered, at room temperature for up to 3 days or frozen for
up to 1 month.

Udon in Broth with Wasabi and Crunchy Vegetables

In Japan, classic dashi is made with dried kelp and dried bonito shavings, but even there, many people now use a powdered dashi stock mix. Dashi powder is available here in many Asian markets. Use it according to the instructions on the label—usually about ½ teaspoon powder to 1 cup of water.

Wasabi, a fiery-hot green horseradish, is usually available in powder form here. To reconstitute it to a paste, mix it about half and half with water.

4 to 6 Servings

---

1 recipe Japanese Udon Noodles	1 tablespoon sugar
1 teaspoon dashi powder	½ cup chopped scallions
¼ cup soy sauce	1 to 2 tablespoons wasabi paste
3 tablespoons mirin (Japanese sweet rice wine) or dry sherry	1 cup shredded carrots
	¾ cup shredded daikon

---

1. Cut the noodle dough into spaghetti. Let dry on wax paper for at least 15 minutes before cooking. Cook in a large pot of boiling salted water until tender but still firm, 2 to 3 minutes. Drain in a colander.

2. Make the dashi in a small saucepan by stirring the powder into 2 cups water over medium heat until the powder dissolves, about 1 minute. Add the soy sauce, mirin, and sugar and stir until the sugar dissolves, about 1 minute. Stir in the chopped scallions.

3. Transfer the noodles to bowls and add a few tablespoons of the dashi to each bowl. Pass the remaining dashi and the wasabi, carrots, and daikon at the table so that guests can add their own to taste.

Glazed Teriyaki Pork and Udon Noodles

4 to 6 Servings

⅓ cup vegetable oil

¼ cup soy sauce

¼ cup dry sherry

½ cup finely chopped scallions

2 garlic cloves, crushed through a press

1 tablespoon sugar

1 pound boneless pork chops

1 recipe Japanese Udon Noodles

1 pound broccoli florets

2 tablespoons chopped pickled ginger

---

1. In a small bowl, combine the oil, soy sauce, sherry, scallions, garlic, and sugar. Stir until the sugar dissolves. Place the pork chops in a shallow roasting pan and spoon 3 tablespoons of the sauce over them. Turn to coat the chops on both sides and set aside at cool room temperature for at least 15 minutes or for up to 3 hours.

2. Meanwhile, cut the noodle dough into spaghetti. Let dry on wax paper for 15 minutes before using.

3. Preheat the oven to 350 degrees. Roast the pork chops, uncovered, turning once and brushing with the drippings, until glazed outside and no longer pink in the center, 25 to 30 minutes.

4. Cook the noodles in a large pot of boiling salted water until tender but still firm, 2 to 3 minutes. Add the broccoli florets during the last 1 minute of cooking. Drain the noodles and broccoli in a colander and return to the cooking pot.

5. Pour the remaining teriyaki sauce over the noodles and toss to coat. Slice the pork across the grain into thin strips. Add the pork and any cooking juices to the noodles and toss again. Add the ginger, toss, and serve.

Japanese Mushroom-Sesame Udon Noodle Soup

4 Servings

½ recipe Japanese Udon Noodles
4 teaspoons dashi powder
3 tablespoons soy sauce
3 tablespoons mirin (Japanese sweet rice
   wine) or dry sherry

1 tablespoon sugar
6 fresh shiitake mushrooms, stemmed,
   caps thinly sliced
¼ cup minced scallions
1 tablespoon toasted sesame seeds

---

1. Cut the noodles into spaghetti. Let dry on wax paper for at least 15 minutes before using. Cook in a large pot of boiling salted water until tender but still firm, 2 to 3 minutes. Drain in a colander and rinse under cool water to remove excess starch; drain well.

2. In a large saucepan or soup pot, combine the dashi powder and 8 cups of water and stir over medium heat until the powder dissolves. Add the soy sauce, mirin, and sugar and stir until the sugar dissolves, about 1 minute. Add the mushrooms and simmer over medium heat until the mushrooms are somewhat softened, about 5 minutes. Stir in the scallions.

3. Add the cooked noodles to the soup and heat through, 2 to 3 minutes. Ladle the soup into bowls, sprinkle on the sesame seeds, and serve hot.

Japanese Soba Noodles

*Buckwheat flour lends its pleasantly nutty flavor and pale beige color to these tradi-
tional Japanese noodles.*

Makes 1 pound; recommended for thin spaghetti, spaghetti, and linguine

2¼ cups all-purpose bleached or unbleached flour
¾ cup buckwheat flour

1 teaspoon salt
About ¾ cup water

1. Measure the flours by scooping into a measuring cup and leveling off with the back
of a knife. Sift the flours into the mixing container of the pasta machine along with
the salt.

2. Start the machine and slowly pour ¾ cup water into the mixing container. Process,
adding additional water by tablespoons if necessary, and extrude as directed in the machine's manual.

3. Spread the noodles out on wax paper or kitchen towels and sprinkle lightly with flour
to prevent sticking. Let dry for at least 15 minutes or for up to 8 hours before using.
The noodles can be stored, covered, at room temperature for up to 2 days or frozen for
up to 1 month.

Grilled Beef on Soba Salad with Pickled Ginger

*ickled ginger, also known as "gari," can be found in jars in Asian markets and in
any large supermarkets.

to 6 Servings

---

1 recipe Japanese Soba Noodles
3 tablespoons red wine vinegar
2 tablespoons soy sauce
1 tablespoon mirin (Japanese sweet rice
  wine) or dry sherry
2 garlic cloves, crushed through a press
1 teaspoon freshly ground pepper

6 tablespoons peanut or vegetable oil
1 tablespoon Asian sesame oil
¾ pound boneless sirloin steak
1 large bunch of watercress
2 carrots, peeled and cut into thin slices
6 scallions, chopped
2 tablespoons pickled ginger slices

---

1. Cut the noodle dough into linguine. Let dry on wax paper for at least 15 minutes before using. Cook in a large pot of boiling salted water until tender but still firm, about 2 minutes. Drain in a colander and rinse under cold water to remove excess starch; drain well.

2. In a small bowl, whisk together the vinegar, soy sauce, mirin, garlic, and pepper. Whisk in the peanut and sesame oils. Brush the steak with 2 teaspoons of this dressing and marinate for at least 15 minutes. Toss the noodles with the remaining dressing.

3. Prepare a medium-hot fire in a charcoal or gas grill. Grill the beef, turning once, until rare to medium-rare, 4 to 8 minutes total, depending on thickness. Remove to a cutting board and let stand about 5 minutes.

4. Meanwhile, make a bed of watercress on a serving platter. Toss the noodles again, spread them out over the watercress, and sprinkle the sliced carrots on top. Thinly slice the steak across the grain. Arrange the slices of beef over the carrots. Sprinkle the scallions over the salad and top with the pickled ginger. Toss at the table before serving.

Wood-Grilled Vegetables on Soba Salad

4 to 6 Servings

1 recipe Japanese Soba Noodles
⅔ cup peanut or vegetable oil
⅓ cup rice wine vinegar
¼ cup finely chopped fresh ginger
3 garlic cloves, crushed through a press
3 tablespoons tamari or soy sauce
1 tablespoon Asian sesame oil
½ teaspoon crushed hot pepper flakes

1 narrow Japanese eggplant, halved
   lengthwise
1 small red bell pepper, cut into thin,
   2-inch-long strips
1 small yellow bell pepper, cut into thin,
   2-inch-long strips
1 bunch of scallions, thinly sliced
⅓ cup toasted sesame seeds

1. Cut the noodle dough into linguine. Let dry on wax paper for at least 15 minutes before cooking. Cook in a large pot of boiling salted water until tender but still firm, 2 to 3 minutes. Drain in a colander. Rinse with cold water to remove excess starch; drain well.

2. Prepare a medium-hot fire in a charcoal or gas grill. Soak a handful of hickory or other hardwood chips in water for 20 minutes.

3. In a small bowl, whisk together the oil, vinegar, ginger, garlic, soy sauce, sesame oil, and hot pepper. In a shallow dish, toss the vegetables with 3 tablespoons of the dressing. Reserve the remaining dressing.

4. Add the wood chips to the fire according to the manufacturer's instructions. Grill the eggplant and bell peppers, turning occasionally, until softened and lightly charred, about 8 minutes.

5. Toss the cooked noodles with the reserved dressing. Cut the grilled vegetables into bite-size chunks and toss with the noodles. Sprinkle with the scallions and sesame seeds. Serve warm or at room temperature.

Hot Soba Noodles with Vegetables, Tofu, and Ginger-Lime Sauce

4 to 6 Servings

1 recipe Japanese Soba Noodles
6 tablespoons peanut or vegetable oil
2 tablespoons minced fresh ginger
3 garlic cloves, crushed through a press
3 tablespoons soy sauce
3 tablespoons lime juice

1 tablespoon chili oil
1¾ cups vegetable broth
3 cups shredded spinach leaves
1½ cups frozen peas, thawed
2 cups diced firm tofu (10 ounces)
1 bunch of scallions, thinly sliced

1. Cut the noodle dough into thin linguine. Let dry on wax paper for at least 15 minutes. Cook in a large pot of boiling salted water until tender but still firm, about 2 minutes. Drain in a colander.

2. In a large skillet, heat the oil over medium heat. Add the ginger and garlic and cook until fragrant, about 30 seconds. Remove from the heat and stir in the soy sauce, lime juice, and chili oil.

3. Add the cooked noodles, broth, spinach, and peas to the pan. Cook, tossing occasionally, until the noodles are heated through and the spinach is wilted, about 2 minutes. Add the tofu and stir gently so it does not crumble. Sprinkle the scallions on top and serve.

Chicken Pad Thai

Make this hot sweet-and-sour Thai restaurant favorite at home either with tender rice noodles or with fresh Chinese egg noodles.

4 Servings

---

3 tablespoons Thai fish sauce (*nam pla*)
2 tablespoons tomato paste
1 tablespoon sugar
1 tablespoon rice wine vinegar
½ teaspoon crushed hot pepper flakes
1 cup reduced-sodium chicken broth or water
½ recipe Asian Rice Noodles
2 tablespoons peanut or vegetable oil

2 eggs
¾ pound skinless, boneless chicken breast, cut into ½-inch cubes
2 garlic cloves, crushed through a press
2 cups bean sprouts
1 red bell pepper, chopped
½ cup chopped roasted peanuts
1 bunch of scallions, thinly sliced
1 lime, cut into wedges

---

1. In a small bowl, whisk together the fish sauce, tomato paste, sugar, vinegar, and hot pepper. Whisk in the broth or water and set this sauce mixture aside.

2. Cut the noodle dough into spaghetti. Let dry on wax paper for at least 15 minutes. Cook in a large pot of boiling salted water until tender but still firm, 2 to 3 minutes. Drain in a colander and rinse with cold water to remove the starch; drain well.

3. Heat 1 teaspoon of the oil in a large skillet over medium heat. Lightly beat the eggs with 2 teaspoons of water, pour into the skillet, and swirl to film the bottom of the skillet. Cook until the egg pancake is set and the bottom is pale golden, 1 to 2 minutes. Peel out of the skillet and cut into thin strips about 2 inches long.

4. Heat the remaining oil in the skillet or a wok over high heat. Add the chicken and stir-fry until white throughout but still juicy, about 2 minutes. Add the garlic and stir-fry until fragrant, about 30 seconds. Add the reserved sauce mixture and cook, stirring, until it boils and thickens, about 1 minute.

5. Reduce the heat to medium and add the cooked noodles, egg pancake, and bean sprouts. Toss until the noodles are coated with sauce and heated through, 2 to 3 minutes. Serve hot. Pass the chopped red bell pepper, peanuts, scallions, and lime wedges separately at the table.

Shrimp and Tofu Pad Thai

4 Servings

3 tablespoons Thai fish sauce (*nam pla*)
2 tablespoons tomato paste
1 tablespoon sugar
1 tablespoon rice wine vinegar
½ teaspoon crushed hot pepper flakes
1 cup reduced-sodium chicken broth or water
½ recipe Asian Rice Noodles
2 tablespoons peanut or vegetable oil
6 ounces firm tofu, cut into ½-inch dice

¾ pound medium shrimp, shelled and deveined
¾ cup thinly sliced scallions
2 cups bean sprouts
½ cup chopped roasted peanuts
½ cup cilantro sprigs
1 lemon, cut into wedges
1 fresh jalapeño or red chile, seeded and minced (optional)

1. In a small bowl, whisk together the fish sauce, tomato paste, sugar, vinegar, and hot pepper. Whisk in the broth or water and set this sauce mixture aside.

2. Cut the noodle dough into spaghetti. Let dry on wax paper for at least 15 minutes. Cook in a large pot of boiling salted water until tender but still firm, 2 to 3 minutes. Drain in a colander and rinse with cold water to remove the starch; drain well.

3. In a large skillet or wok, heat the oil over high heat. Add the tofu and stir-fry until the surface is golden, 1 to 2 minutes. Remove with a slotted spoon.

4. Add the shrimp and scallions to the same pan and stir-fry until the shrimp are pink and curled, about 2 minutes. Add the reserved sauce mixture and cook, stirring, until it boils, about 1 minute.

5. Reduce the heat to medium and add the cooked noodles, tofu, and bean sprouts. Toss until the noodles are coated with sauce and heated through, 2 to 3 minutes. Serve hot. Pass the peanuts, cilantro, lemon wedges, and minced chile separately at the table.

Asian Rice Noodles

Rice noodles are extremely popular all over Asia, where they are usually sold dried. This fresh version is made with rice flour, which is available in health food stores, and high-gluten bread flour. Rice noodles make a particularly delicious foil for all kinds of flavorful Asian sauces.

Makes 1 pound; recommended for Asian noodles, thin spaghetti, spaghetti, and linguine

---

2 cups bread flour	1 teaspoon salt
1 cup white rice flour	About ¾ cup water

---

1. Measure the flours by scooping them into a measuring cup and leveling them off with the back of a knife. Sift the flours into the mixing container of the pasta machine along with the salt.

2. Start the machine and slowly pour ¾ cup water into the mixing container. Process, adding additional water by tablespoons if necessary, and extrude as directed in the machine's manual.

3. Spread the noodles out on wax paper or kitchen towels and sprinkle lightly with rice flour to prevent sticking. Let dry for at least 15 minutes or for up to 2 hours before cooking. Rice noodles can be stored in the refrigerator for up to 24 hours but freezing is not recommended.

Tangy Thai Noodle Soup

4 Servings

---

3 tablespoons Thai fish sauce (*nam pla*)
1 tablespoon tomato paste
1 tablespoon peanut or vegetable oil
1 tablespoon sugar
1 tablespoon lime juice
2 garlic cloves, crushed through a press
½ to ¾ teaspoon crushed hot pepper
    flakes

½ recipe Asian Rice Noodles
10 cups chicken broth, preferably reduced-
    sodium
3 celery ribs, thinly sliced
½ cup chopped cilantro

---

1. To make the sauce, whisk together the fish sauce, tomato paste, oil, sugar, lime juice, garlic, and hot pepper. Set aside for at least 30 minutes so the flavors can blend.

2. Cut the noodle dough into thin spaghetti. Let dry on wax paper for at least 15 minutes before using.

3. In a large soup pot, bring the broth to a boil over high heat. Add the noodles and celery and simmer until the noodles are tender, 2 to 3 minutes. Stir in the cilantro.

4. Ladle the soup into bowls. Pass the sauce at the table so that each person can add it to taste.

Asian Rice Noodles

Crispy Thai Noodle Pancake with Garnishes

This crunchy Thai-flavored pancake can serve as a light vegetarian main course or as an accompaniment to grilled meats. It's also delicious made with thin fresh egg noodles.

4 Servings

½ recipe Asian Rice Noodles

2 eggs

½ cup chopped scallions

1 tablespoon Thai fish sauce (*nam pla*)

½ teaspoon cayenne

2 tablespoons flour

1½ tablespoons peanut or vegetable oil

1 teaspoon Asian sesame oil

1½ cups plain yogurt

⅓ cup chopped cilantro

1 red bell pepper, chopped

1 lime, cut into wedges

---

1. Cut the noodle dough into regular or thin spaghetti. Let dry on wax paper for 15 minutes before cooking. Cook in a large pot of boiling salted water until tender but still firm, about 2 minutes. Drain in a colander and rinse with cold water to remove excess starch.

2. In a large bowl, whisk the eggs with the scallions, fish sauce, and cayenne. Add the noodles, sprinkle with the flour, and toss to coat evenly.

3. In a large (10- to 11-inch) skillet, preferably nonstick, heat the peanut and sesame oils over medium heat. Add the noodle mixture, pressing it evenly into the pan. Cover and cook until crispy and browned on the bottom, 3 to 5 minutes.

4. Cut the pancake into 4 quarters. Turn each quarter with a spatula and cook until the eggs are set and the second side is lightly browned, 2 to 3 minutes.

5. In a small bowl, whisk the yogurt with the chopped cilantro. Pass it at the table, along with the chopped red bell pepper and lime wedges as garnishes for the pancake.

Plain Bread Sticks

It's fun to watch the pasta machine knead and shape bread dough for bread sticks. It takes a bit longer to mix bread dough than it does pasta dough, but a little practice will teach you just when the dough is the correct smooth consistency for extruding.

Makes 1 pound; 25 to 30 bread sticks

---

3 cups bread flour
1 envelope rapid-rise yeast (2 teaspoons)
1 teaspoon salt

1 teaspoon sugar
¼ cup olive oil
1 cup hot water (about 120 degrees)

---

1. Measure the flour by scooping it into a measuring cup and leveling it off with the back of a knife. Sift it into the mixing container of the pasta machine. Add the yeast, salt, and sugar to the container and mix until well blended.

2. Start the machine and slowly pour the oil and water into the mixing container. Process for 3 minutes, adding additional water or flour by tablespoons if needed, until the dough is almost smooth and begins to clump together into small balls. Using the bread stick attachment, extrude according to the machine's manual.

3. Cut the dough into 6-inch lengths. On a lightly floured surface, use the palms of your hands to roll each piece of dough to a 9- or 10-inch length. Place the bread sticks 1 inch apart on ungreased baking sheets and set aside in a warm place for 30 minutes, or until slightly risen.

4. Preheat the oven to 375 degrees. Bake the bread sticks until pale golden brown and crisp, 15 to 20 minutes. Cool on a wire rack. The bread sticks can be stored for 1 day well wrapped in a plastic bag, or frozen for up to 1 month.

Herbed Black Pepper Bread Sticks

These herb- and pepper-flecked bread sticks make a fabulous hors d'oeuvre. We like to serve them with a soft goat cheese.

Makes 25 to 30 bread sticks

---

3 cups bread flour
1 envelope rapid-rise yeast (2 teaspoons)
1 tablespoon coarsely ground black pepper
2 teaspoons finely crumbled dried herbs, such as basil, rosemary, thyme, sage, and/or marjoram

1 teaspoon salt
1 teaspoon sugar
¼ cup olive oil
1 cup hot water (about 120 degrees)

---

1. Measure the flour by scooping it into a measuring cup and leveling it off with the back of a knife. Sift it into the mixing container of the pasta machine. Add the yeast, pepper, herbs, salt, and sugar to the container and mix until well blended.

2. Start the machine and slowly pour the oil and water into the mixing container. Process for 3 minutes, adding additional water or flour by tablespoons if needed, until the dough is almost smooth and begins to clump together into small balls. Using the bread stick attachment, extrude the dough according to the machine's manual.

3. Cut the dough into 6-inch lengths. On a lightly floured surface, use the palms of your hands to roll each piece of dough into a 9- or 10-inch length. Place the bread sticks 1 inch apart on ungreased baking sheets and set aside in a warm place for 30 minutes, or until slightly risen.

4. Preheat the oven to 375 degrees. Bake the bread sticks until pale golden brown and crisp, 15 to 20 minutes. Cool on a wire rack. The bread sticks can be stored for 1 day well wrapped in a plastic bag, or frozen for up to 1 month.

Parmesan Bread Sticks

Serve these crisp, cheese-flavored bread sticks as a snack or with almost any soup or pasta dish.

Makes 25 to 30 bread sticks

---

3 cups bread flour
½ cup grated Parmesan cheese
1 envelope rapid-rise yeast (2 teaspoons)
1 teaspoon salt

1 teaspoon sugar
¼ teaspoon cayenne
¼ cup olive oil
1 cup hot water (about 120 degrees)

---

1. Measure the flour by scooping it into a measuring cup and leveling it off with the back of a knife. Sift it into the mixing container of the pasta machine. Add the cheese, yeast, salt, sugar, and cayenne to the container and mix until well blended.

2. Start the machine and slowly pour the oil and water into the mixing container. Process for 3 minutes, adding additional water or flour by tablespoons if needed, until the dough is almost smooth and begins to clump together into small balls. Using the bread stick attachment, extrude the dough according to the machine's manual.

3. Cut the dough into 6-inch lengths. On a lightly floured surface, use the palms of your hands to roll each piece of dough into a 9- or 10-inch length. Place the bread sticks 1 inch apart on ungreased baking sheets and set aside in a warm place for 30 minutes, or until slightly risen.

4. Preheat the oven to 375 degrees. Bake the bread sticks until pale golden brown and crisp, 15 to 20 minutes. Cool on a wire rack. The bread sticks can be stored for 1 day well wrapped in a plastic bag, or frozen for up to 1 month.

Salted Bread Sticks

We like to serve these with cocktails. They look particularly striking when presented fanned out of a tall glass.

Makes 25 to 30 bread sticks

---

3 cups bread flour
1 envelope rapid-rise yeast (2 teaspoons)
½ teaspoon salt
1 teaspoon sugar
¼ cup olive oil

1 cup hot water (about 120 degrees)
1 egg yolk, lightly beaten with 2 teaspoons water
About 2 tablespoons coarse kosher salt or sea salt

---

1. Measure the flour by scooping it into a measuring cup and leveling it off with the back of a knife. Sift it into the mixing container of the pasta machine. Add the yeast, salt, and sugar to the container and mix until well blended.

2. Start the machine and slowly pour the oil and water into the mixing container. Process for 3 minutes, adding additional water or flour by tablespoons if needed, until the dough is almost smooth and begins to clump together into small balls. Using the bread stick attachment, extrude according to the machine's manual.

3. Cut the dough into 6-inch lengths. On a lightly floured surface, use the palms of your hands to roll each piece of dough into a 9- or 10-inch length. Place the bread sticks 1 inch apart on ungreased baking sheets and set aside in a warm place for 30 minutes, or until slightly risen.

4. Preheat the oven to 375 degrees. Using a small brush, paint the tops of the bread sticks with the egg wash and sprinkle heavily with the salt.

5. Bake the bread sticks in the preheated oven until pale golden and crisp, 15 to 20 minutes. Cool on a wire rack. The bread sticks can be stored for 1 day well wrapped in a plastic bag, or frozen for up to 1 month.

Whole Wheat Bread Sticks

These nutty, whole wheat bread sticks are wonderful served with soups or salads. For a delicious twist, brush the bread sticks with an egg wash and sprinkle with sesame seeds just before they go into the oven.

Makes 25 to 30 bread sticks

---

2 cups bread flour
1 cup whole wheat flour
1 envelope rapid-rise yeast (2 teaspoons)
1 teaspoon salt

¼ cup olive oil
1 tablespoon molasses
1 cup hot water (about 120 degrees)

---

1. Measure the flours by scooping them into a measuring cup and leveling them off with the back of a knife. Sift the flours into the mixing container of the pasta machine. Add the yeast and salt and mix until well blended.

2. Combine the olive oil and molasses in a measuring cup. Start the machine and slowly pour the oil and molasses mixture and the water into the mixing container. Process for about 3 minutes, adding additional water or flour by tablespoons if needed, until the dough is almost smooth and begins to clump together into small balls. Using the bread stick attachment, extrude according to the machine's manual.

3. Cut the dough into 6-inch lengths. On a lightly floured surface, use the palms of your hands to roll each piece of dough into a 9- or 10-inch length. Place the bread sticks 1 inch apart on ungreased baking sheets and set aside in a warm place for 30 minutes, or until slightly risen.

4. Preheat the oven to 375 degrees. Bake the bread sticks until pale golden brown and crisp, 15 to 20 minutes. Cool on a wire rack. The bread sticks can be stored for 1 day well wrapped in a plastic bag, or frozen for up to 1 month.

Chocolate Pasta

Use your pasta machine to make this surprisingly delicious dessert pasta.

Makes 1 pound; use for fettuccine or linguine

2¾ cups all-purpose flour
½ cup unsweetened cocoa powder
½ cup sugar

¼ teaspoon salt
3 "large" eggs
Milk

---

1. Measure the flour by scooping it into a measuring cup and leveling it off with the back of a knife. Sift it into the mixing container of the pasta machine along with the cocoa, sugar, and salt.

2. Break the eggs into a liquid measuring cup. Add enough milk to make ¾ cup. Use a fork or small whisk to lightly beat the eggs.

3. Start the machine and slowly pour the liquid into the mixing container. Process, adding additional milk by tablespoons if needed, until the dough begins to clump together. Extrude as directed in the machine's manual.

4. Spread the pasta out on wax paper or kitchen towels. Let dry for at least 15 minutes or for up to 2 hours before using. The pasta can be stored in the refrigerator for up to 24 hours.

Chocolate Fettuccine "Sundaes"

This novelty sweet will delight dessert lovers of all ages. Not only does it sound and look intriguing, it really tastes delicious.

6 Servings

---

1 recipe Chocolate Pasta
½ cup chopped pecans
1 cup heavy cream
8 ounces chopped semisweet chocolate or
  chocolate chips

2 tablespoons dark rum
1 teaspoon vanilla extract
6 maraschino cherries

---

1. Preheat the oven to 350 degrees. Cut the pasta into fettuccine. Let dry on wax paper for at least 15 minutes before using.

2. Meanwhile, spread the nuts on a small baking sheet and toast 5 to 7 minutes, stirring once or twice, until fragrant and lightly browned.

3. For the sauce, in a heavy, medium saucepan, bring the cream to a boil over medium-high heat. Remove from the heat, add the chocolate, and stir until the chocolate melts and the sauce is smooth. Stir in the rum and vanilla.

4. Cook the fettuccine in a large pot of rapidly boiling water until tender but still firm, about 2 minutes. Drain in a colander.

5. Transfer the fettuccine to dessert plates. Drizzle the warm chocolate sauce over the pasta. Sprinkle the toasted pecans on top. To complete the sundae effect, garnish each dessert with a maraschino cherry and serve.

Sweet Marsala Pasta

This slightly sweet dough is used to make delectable Italian-style cookies and pastries.

Makes 1 pound; use to make lasagne strips for cookies and pastries

---

3 cups all-purpose flour
3 tablespoons confectioners' sugar
¼ teaspoon salt

6 tablespoons unsalted butter, softened
3 "large" eggs
¼ to ⅓ cup Marsala or other sweet wine

---

1. Measure the flour by scooping it into a measuring cup and leveling it off with the back of a knife. Sift it into the mixing container of the pasta machine along with the sugar and salt. Cut the butter into small pieces, distribute over the flour, and turn the machine on to mix until the butter is evenly distributed.

2. Break the eggs into a liquid measuring cup. Add enough Marsala to make ¾ cup. Use a fork or small whisk to lightly beat the eggs.

3. Start the machine and slowly pour the liquid into the mixing container. Process, adding additional wine by tablespoons if needed, until the dough begins to clump together. Extrude as directed in the machine's manual.

4. Loosely cover the dough with plastic wrap or a kitchen towel until ready to use.

Crisp-Fried Sweet Cheese Pastries

Makes about 30 pastries

---

1 recipe Sweet Marsala Pasta
All-purpose flour
1½ cups ricotta cheese
⅔ cup confectioners' sugar
⅔ cup chopped almonds, preferably lightly toasted

½ cup semisweet chocolate chips, coarsely chopped
¾ teaspoon grated lemon zest
Vegetable oil
Confectioners' sugar

---

1. Cut the pasta into lasagne noodles about 6 inches long. Dust lightly with flour and use a rolling pin or hand-cranked pasta machine to make sheets about 3 inches wide and 9 inches long. You should have 20 sheets. Save any leftover dough for another use. Cover loosely with plastic wrap until ready to shape.

2. In a mixing bowl, stir together the ricotta, confectioners' sugar, almonds, chocolate chips, and lemon zest.

3. Place a pasta sheet on a flat work surface. Spoon 3 evenly spaced mounds of cheese filling on the pasta sheet, using a rounded teaspoonful for each mound. Dip a pastry brush in water and moisten the dough around each mound of filling. Cover with another pasta sheet and seal between the mounds by pressing gently with your finger. Use a knife or fluted pastry wheel to cut apart. Press the edges together firmly to seal. Repeat with the remaining dough and filling. Let dry on a rack for 30 minutes or refrigerate for up to 4 hours.

4. Heat about 1 inch of oil in a large, heavy skillet over medium heat to 350 degrees. Add the pastries to the hot oil a few at a time and cook until golden on both sides, 1 to 1½ minutes. Drain on paper towels. Sprinkle with confectioners' sugar. Although the pastries are at their very best when warm, they can also be served at room temperature. Store, loosely wrapped, at cool room temperature for up to 24 hours.

Sugared Marsala Bow Knots

These celebratory Italian pastries are often made for carnivals or other outdoor festivals, where the frying is done outdoors. They make a fabulous treat.

Makes about 3 dozen bow knots

---

1 recipe Sweet Marsala Pasta
All-purpose flour

Vegetable oil
Confectioners' sugar

---

1. Cut the pasta into lasagne noodles about 7 inches long. Sprinkle lightly with flour and use a rolling pin or hand-cranked pasta machine to make sheets about 11 inches long.
2. Heat approximately 2 inches of oil in a large, heavy skillet over medium heat to 350 degrees.
3. Trim the dough into strips approximately 5 inches long and ¾ inch wide. Make a 1-inch slit near one end of each strip and gently pull the other end of the strip through the hole to make a loose loop.
4. Fry the pastries, a few at a time, until pale golden on both sides, about 1 minute. Drain on paper towels. Sprinkle heavily with confectioners' sugar. Serve warm or at room temperature, heaped on a platter.

Index

Broccoli, roasted, low-fat penne with, 29

Broccoli rabe, sun-dried tomato rigatoni with white beans and, 135

Broth, udon in, with wasabi and crunchy vegetables, 163

Brunswick stew over carrot noodles, 62

Cabbage, Savoy, in summer minestrone with basil and garlic pasta, 36

Cajun pasta, 53
fettuccine with French Quarter shrimp creole, 56
penne with chunky chicken sauce piquante, 54
spaghettini with crawfish court bouillon sauce, 58
spaghetti with bayou andouille sauce, 57

Calamari sauce, peppery, spaghetti neri with, 107

Cannelloni, saffron, with four cheeses, 118

Capellini
beet, with scallops and smoked ham, 44
carrot, with parsley-dill pesto, 61
neri with shrimp and toasted bread crumbs, 104
spinach, with parslied white clam sauce, 130
tarragon, primavera, 86
wild mushroom, with prosciutto and roasted pepper puree, 146

Capers, lemon spaghettini with smoked salmon and, 102

Caponata, whole wheat linguine with, 31

Carbonara, sun-dried tomato spaghetti, 138

Carrot pasta, 60
capellini with parsley-dill pesto, 61
noodles, Brunswick stew over, 62
rigatoni, Peter Rabbit's, 63
ziti ratatouille, 64

Cheddar and ale sauce, tomato macaroni with, 142

Cheese(s)
Cheddar, and ale sauce, tomato macaroni with, 142
cilantro macaroni and, Susan's baked, 70
mozzarella, smoked, and plum tomato sauce, scallion penne with, 125
Parmesan bread sticks, 178
pastries, crisp-fried sweet, 184
Pecorino Romano, potato gnocchi gratineed with sage and, 115
saffron cannelloni with four, 118
in Southwest-style cilantro lasagne, 68
in wild mushroom lasagne with sun-dried tomato pasta, 136

Chicken
in Brunswick stew over carrot noodles, 62
cacciatore over wild mushroom spaghetti, 149
egg noodle soup, Nana's, 22
noodle salad
with lemongrass vinaigrette, 156

with lime-mint dressing, Vietnamese, 154
pad Thai, 170
pot stickers, curried, 158
sauce piquante, chunky, Cajun penne with, 54

Chickpeas (garbanzo beans)
and eggplant spinach spaghetti, Mediterranean, 132
tomato ziti with Mediterranean lamb, zucchini, and, 144

Chile, chorizo, and corn sauce, New Mexican, cilantro linguine with, 67

Chili
sauce, pork and black bean, cilantro rigatoni with, 72
spaghetti, Cincinnati, 48
turkey, low-fat, with macaroni, 27

Chinese egg noodle(s), 150
in chicken noodle salad with lemongrass vinaigrette, 156
cold sesame, 152
in curried chicken pot stickers, 158
salad, cold peanut, 153
stir-fried pork and black bean sauce with, 151
in Szechuan shrimp dumplings with fireball dipping sauce, 160
in Vietnamese chicken noodle salad with lime-mint dressing, 154

Chocolate pasta, 181
fettuccine "sundaes," 182

Chorizo
corn, and chile sauce, New Mexican, cilantro linguine with, 67
and pepper sauce, fiesta, saffron penne with, 120

Choucroute sauce, Alsatian, egg noodles in, 23

Cilantro pasta, 65
frittata, curried squash and pepper, 66
lasagne, Southwest-style, 68
linguine with New Mexican chorizo, corn, and chile sauce, 67
macaroni and cheese, Susan's baked, 70
rigatoni with pork and black bean chili sauce, 72

Cincinnati chili spaghetti, 48

Cioppino with saffron linguine, 117

Citrus, dill spaghettini with scallops and, 79

Clam sauce
parslied white, spinach capellini with, 130
robust red, black pepper linguine with, 51

Cleaning up after making pasta, 7–8

Cold peanut noodle salad, 153

Cold sesame noodles, Chinese, 152

Consistency of pasta (texture), 4

Cooking times for fresh pasta, 6

Corn, chorizo, and chile sauce, New Mexican, cilantro linguine with, 67